Nicholas Felton

PHOTOVIZ

Visualizing Information
Through Photography

gestalten

WHAT IS PHOTOVIZ?

BY
NICHOLAS FELTON

1.

I DON'T OVER-THINK THE PROJECTS I SHARE ON MY BLOG (FELTRON.TUMBLR.COM). THE ENTRIES INSPIRE ME AND LOOSELY RELATE TO DATA VISUALIZATION. SOME OF THE IMAGES ARE FORMALLY INTERESTING, OTHERS ARE CONCEPTUALLY EXCITING, AND THE MAJORITY ARE BOTH. WHAT SURPRISED ME IS HOW MANY OF THESE PROJECTS SUCCEED AS A VISUALIZATION, BUT ARE ANCHORED IN PHOTOGRAPHY RATHER THAN DATA. THIS INTERSECTION IS SOMETHING I HAVE COME TO THINK OF AS "PHOTOVIZ": IMAGES THAT COMBINE THE LARGER NARRATIVES OF VISUALIZATIONS WITH THE IMMEDIACY OF PHOTOGRAPHY.

CONSIDER A TYPICAL PHOTOGRAPH OF A POLE VAULTER IN WHICH THE ATHLETE FLOATS, FROZEN IN THE MIDDLE OF A COMPLEX MOVEMENT. THE PHOTO REVEALS THE FITNESS, BALANCE, AND CONCENTRATION REQUIRED OF THE ATHLETE IN THIS INSTANT.[1]

A DIAGRAM OF THE MOVEMENTS ILLUSTRATES THE POLE VAULT SEQUENCE FROM START TO FINISH. THIS APPROACH TELLS A LONGER STORY AND ALLOWS FOR COMPARISON OF THE COMPLEX MOVEMENTS, BUT SACRIFICES DETAIL AND SPECIFICITY.[2] USING A TECHNIQUE CALLED STROBOSCOPY, HAROLD E. EDGERTON WAS ABLE TO COMBINE THE STEPS OF THE DIAGRAM WITH PHOTOGRAPHIC PRECISION TO

pole vault

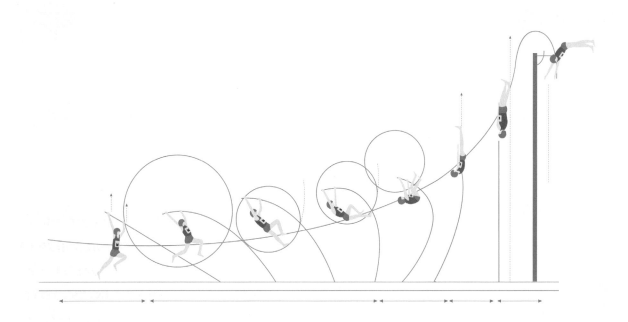

2.
HELGA JUÁREZ
Pole Vault

ILLUSTRATE THE MOVEMENTS OF THE POLE VAULT-ER. THIS REPRESENTATION DEMONSTRATES HOW THE GOALS OF BOTH DATA VISUALIZATION AND PHOTOG-RAPHY CAN COEXIST AND CREATE SOMETHING MORE INFORMATIVE AND EXPRESSIVE.

DATA VISUALIZATION IS THE GRAPHIC REPRESEN-TATION OF INFORMATION. TRANSFORMING DATA INTO A VISUAL FORM MAKES IT MORE ACCESSIBLE AND AL-LOWS FOR BETTER COMPARISONS AND UNDERSTAND-ING. IN GENERAL TERMS, DATA IS INFORMATION IN A FORM THAT IS USEFUL FOR PROCESSING; THIS COULD MEAN NUMBERS, DESCRIPTIONS, RELATIONSHIPS, OR EVEN PHOTOGRAPHS.

A PHOTOGRAPH TAKES THE CHAOTIC, TANGIBLE, MULTI-DIMENSIONAL WORLD AND REDUCES IT INTO SOMETHING FLAT AND STILL. A PHOTOGRAPH RE-MAINS A COMPLEX OBJECT—WHETHER CONSIDERED

AS MILLIONS OF PIXELS OR AS WORTH A PROVERBIAL "THOUSAND WORDS"—BUT BY BOTH MEASURES IT IS VASTLY SIMPLER THAN THE MOMENT IT REPRESENTS. LIKE DATA, PHOTOGRAPHY REDUCES THE WORLD'S COMPLEXITY INTO A FORM THAT IS SUITABLE FOR MA-NIPULATION AND DATA VISUALIZATION.

BY COMBINING THE GOALS OF DATA VISUALIZATION WITH THE BEAUTY AND FIDELITY OF PHOTOGRAPHY, PHOTOVIZ IS ABLE TO REPRESENT THE WORLD IN IL-LUMINATING WAYS. THIS COLLECTION RANGES FROM SINGLE PHOTOS THAT EXPRESS AGGREGATE STORIES, TO NOVEL PHOTOGRAPHIC TECHNIQUES THAT EXPAND PERCEPTION, TO VISUALIZATIONS CONNECTING THOU-SANDS OF PHOTOS. THESE APPROACHES COMPLE-MENT THE INCREASE IN PRODUCTION AND FIDELITY OF PHOTOGRAPHS AND OFFER SOLUTIONS FOR MANAG-ING THE FUTURE FLOOD OF IMAGES.

ORIGINS

/

ON A SPRING MORNING IN PARIS IN 1838, LOUIS DAGUERRE MADE HISTORY BY CAPTURING WHAT IS WIDELY BE-LIEVED TO BE THE FIRST PHOTOGRAPH OF A PERSON. THE DAGUERREOTYPE HAD NOT YET BEEN PUBLICLY RE-VEALED AND THIS IMAGE WAS PRESENTED ALONGSIDE TWO OTHERS TO PROMOTE HIS INVENTION. "BOULEVARD DU TEMPLE" DEPICTS A PARISIAN STREET DEVOID OF INHABITANTS OR VEHICLES BESIDES THE SINGLE SILHOUETTE OF A MAN EXTENDING HIS FOOT.[3] LIMITS ON THE SENSITIVITY OF DAGUERRE'S PROCESS MEANT THAT THIS IMAGE REQUIRED AN EXPOSURE TIME OF MORE THAN TEN MINUTES AND CAPTURED ONLY MOTIONLESS OBJECTS LIKE THE BUILDINGS, THE STREET AND THIS MAN WHO WAS PROBABLY HAVING HIS SHOES SHINED.

"BOULEVARD DU TEMPLE" IS AS TRUTHFUL AS IT IS MISLEADING. OUR ABILITY TO INTERPRET IMAGES IS LIM-ITED BY OUR SENSES. BECAUSE WE PERCEIVE TIME AS A SERIES OF MOMENTS, WE INSTINCTIVELY ASSUME THAT THIS IMAGE REPRESENTS AN INSTANT. THIS IS AS TRUE TODAY AS IT WAS IN 1838 WHEN SAMUEL MORSE SAW THE IMAGE AND WAS SHOCKED BY THE EMPTINESS OF PARIS. BY CAPTURING A VIEW THAT IS BEYOND THE LIMITS OF OUR SENSES, THE IMAGE REVEALS AN ALTERNATE TRUTH IN WHICH STATIC OBJECTS ARE ISOLATED FROM OB-JECTS IN MOTION.

SINCE THE INVENTION OF THE DAGUERROTYPE, PHOTOGRAPHY HAS PURSUED PARITY WITH OUR PERCEPTION. FASTER SHUTTER SPEEDS, HIGHER RESOLUTION, THE ADDITION OF COLOR, MOTION AND INTERACTIVITY HAVE PUSHED PHOTOGRAPHIC OUTPUT TOWARDS THE LIMITS OF OUR SENSES. THESE ADVANCES MOVED US EVER CLOSER TO THE SUBJECT, TRANSPORTING US THROUGH TIME AND SPACE WITH INCREASING FIDELITY TOWARDS THE ORIGINAL MOMENT.

IMAGING HAS NOW OVERTAKEN OUR EYES, UNLOCKING DISCOVERIES BEYOND THE BOUNDARIES OF HUMAN PERCEPTION. IMPROVEMENTS IN SHUTTER SPEED HAVE DEMYSTIFIED THE MOVEMENT OF A GALLOPING HORSE.[4] AND FROZEN A BULLET IN MID-FLIGHT.[5] TODAY'S FASTEST CAMERA CAN RESOLVE MOMENTS ONLY ONE-TRIL-LIONTH OF A SECOND LONG. MICROSCOPIC IMAGING HAS REVEALED THE FIRST PHOTOGRAPHS OF AN ATOM, THE SMALLEST OBJECT THAT CAN BE SEEN USING VISIBLE LIGHT. OUTSIDE OF THE VISIBLE SPECTRUM, THE INVISIBLE WORLD IS NOW CASUALLY REVEALED USING INFRARED, ULTRAVIOLET, AND X-RAYS.

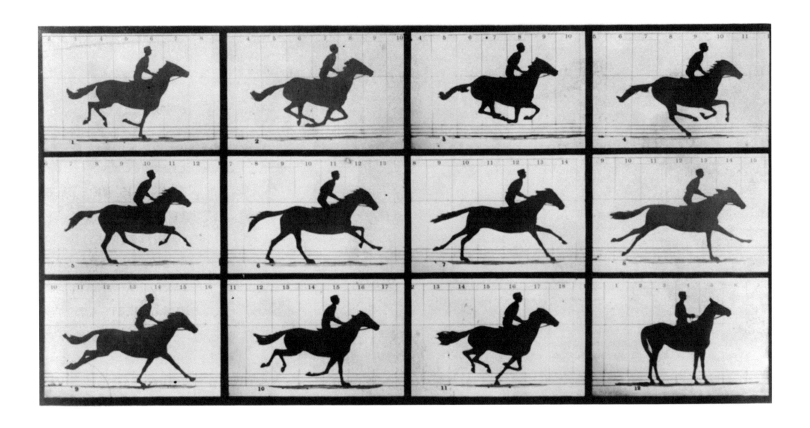

4.
EADWEARD MUYBRIDGE
The Horse in Motion

MOMENTS

/

AS A DOCUMENTARY TOOL, THE PHOTOGRAPH HAS HISTORICALLY BEEN A MARKER OF SIGNIFICANCE, A MEANS OF PRESERVING A NOTEWORTHY MOMENT FOR POSTERITY. WHILE EARLY PHOTOGRAPHS WERE RESERVED FOR NEWSWORTHY EVENTS OR PORTRAITS OF THE WEALTHY AND IMPORTANT, BY 1960 IT IS ESTIMATED THAT 55 PERCENT OF PHOTOS WERE OF BABIES. AS THE AFFORDABILITY AND ACCESSIBILITY OF PHOTOGRAPHY INCREASED, MOMENTS WORTH PHOTOGRAPHING BECAME MORE COMMON AND GENERALLY LESS SIGNIFICANT.

HENRI CARTIER-BRESSON MADE HIS CAREER BY MASTERFULLY OBSERVING AND CAPTURING MOMENTS OF SIGNIFICANCE IN THE MID-TWENTIETH CENTURY. CARTIER-BRESSON CALLED THEM "DECISIVE MOMENTS," AND HIS WORK WAS DEDICATED TO CAPTURING THESE MEANINGFUL EVENTS AND FORMS. HIS PHOTOGRAPHS EXEMPLIFY SOME OF THE GREATEST POTENTIAL OF ONE PHOTOGRAPHER, ONE MOMENT, AND A SINGLE POINT OF VIEW.

CARTIER-BRESSON WAS VERY MUCH A PRODUCT OF HIS TIME. DURING HIS CAREER, MOST MOMENTS WERE NOT CAPTURED BY THE GAZE OF A CAMERA, WHILE TODAY VERY FEW CAN ESCAPE IT. A NEAR-FUTURE SCENARIO IN WHICH OUR LIVES ARE RECORDED BY MULTIPLE ANGLES OF STILL OR MOVING IMAGES IS NOT HARD TO IMAGINE. IN THE CONTINUOUSLY CAPTURED WORLD, THE SEARCH FOR SIGNIFICANCE WILL BECOME A PROCESS OF FINDING THE RIGHT IMAGE INSTEAD OF CAPTURING THE PRECISE MOMENT.

IT IS NOW WORTH ASKING WHETHER FINDING THE "DECISIVE MOMENT" SHOULD REMAIN THE GOAL OF PHOTOGRAPHY. THE COSTS ASSOCIATED WITH SHOOTING, DEVELOPING, PRINTING, AND REPRODUCING PHOTOS ONCE CONSTRAINED THE PRODUCTION OF PHOTOGRAPHY, BUT DIGITAL CAMERAS AND THE INTERNET HAVE ELIMINATED THIS RESTRICTION. UNFETTERED PRODUCTION HAS BEEN TAMED ONLINE BY THE BOTTLENECKS OF APPS AND OUR CAPACITY TO CONSUME. BUT IS IT SUFFICIENT? CAN EDITING, SHARING, AND RANKING MEDIATE THE SCALE OF PHOTOGRAPHY TODAY AND MAKE IT MANAGEABLE?

WHEN EVERYONE IS A PHOTOGRAPHER, CONSTANTLY CAPTURING THE SAME OR SIMILAR MOMENTS, HOW DO WE PROCESS THIS OUTPUT? WHAT TECHNIQUES ARE USEFUL FOR UNDERSTANDING THIS NEW TORRENT OF PHOTOGRAPHY, FOR SEPARATING SIGNIFICANCE FROM EVERYTHING ELSE? TO CAPTURE, DISTILL, AND EXPRESS MEANING IN THE FLOW OF IMAGES BEING PRODUCED, WE NEED TO CONSIDER APPROACHES THAT LOOK BEYOND THE MOMENT.

BIG PHOTO

/

WHAT WAS MIRACULOUS IN 1838 IS NOW COMMON-PLACE. WE ARE AWASH IN IMAGES AND SURROUNDED BY CAMERAS. AS WITH DATA, THE QUANTITY OF IMAGERY PRODUCED TODAY EXCEEDS OUR CAPACITY TO UNDER-STAND IT. IF THE COMPLEXITY OF BIG DATA IS DESCRIBED IN TERMS OF VOLUME, VARIETY, AND VELOCITY, THEN IT IS CLEAR THAT "BIG PHOTO" IS IMMINENT.

VOLUME: 1930 WAS THE FIRST YEAR IN WHICH A BIL-LION PHOTOGRAPHS WERE TAKEN. TODAY, THAT NUM-BER APPROACHES 400 BILLION A YEAR. APPROXIMATELY 10 PERCENT OF ALL PHOTOS EVER TAKEN WERE PRO-DUCED IN THE LAST 12 MONTHS, AND THIS NUMBER WILL ONLY INCREASE WITH THE PROLIFERATION AND UBIQUITY OF CAMERAS IN OUR LIVES.

VARIETY: IT WOULD BE HARD FOR ANY MOMENT OF SIGNIFICANCE TO PASS TODAY WITHOUT PHOTOGRAPH-IC DOCUMENTATION. OVER A BILLION SMART PHONES ARE SOLD EACH YEAR, MOST OF THEM EQUIPPED WITH THE CHEAPEST AND HIGHEST QUALITY CAMERA THAT THEIR OWNER HAS EVER POSSESSED. THE SIZE AND FIDELITY OF THESE CAMERAS HAS ALLOWED THEM TO PROLIFERATE THROUGHOUT OUR ENVIRONMENT AND TO COLONIZE BOTH OBVIOUS AND UNEXPECTED DEVICES. IT IS NOW COMMON TO FIND CAMERAS IN PUBLIC SPAC-ES, PRIVATE RESIDENCES, ON CARS, DRONES, WEAR-ABLES, AND TABLETS. MEANWHILE, DEDICATED DIGITAL CAMERA SALES REMAIN SUBSTANTIAL. THOUGH THIS MARKET HAS DECLINED, SALES OF DIGITAL CAMER-AS TODAY REMAIN STRONGER THAN THE FILM CAMERA MARKET OF THE 1980S.

VELOCITY: THE TRANSITION FROM FILM TO DIG-ITAL PHOTOGRAPHY REMOVED THE LIMIT ON HOW MANY PHOTOS A PERSON MIGHT REASONABLY TAKE. WITHOUT THE EXPENSE OF BUYING FILM OR PAYING FOR DEVELOPMENT THE ONLY CONSIDERATION WAS STORAGE. BETWEEN 1997 AND 2010, THE COST OF A GIGABYTE DROPPED BY A FACTOR OF 1,000, ENABLING CAMERAS, COMPUTERS, AND EVENTUALLY THE CLOUD TO HOLD MORE IMAGES AND REMOVING ANY HESITA-TION TO CAPTURE EVERYTHING. LIMITLESS STORAGE HAS ALLOWED WEARABLE, PERSISTENT CAMERAS TO EMERGE. ONE SUCH DEVICE, THE NARRATIVE CAMERA, CLIPS ONTO YOUR CLOTHING AND AUTOMATICALLY TAKES A PHOTO EVERY 30 SECONDS OR AROUND 2,000 OVER A 16-HOUR DAY. CHEAPER STORAGE HAS EN-ABLED HOME SURVEILLANCE SYSTEMS LIKE DROPCAM TO STORE THE VIDEO EQUIVALENT OF UP TO 80 MIL-LION STILL FRAMES.

THE TECHNIQUES OF PHOTOVIZ HOLD PROMISE FOR DISTILLING SIGNIFICANCE FROM THE MASSIVE PHOTO SETS WE ARE STARTING TO PRODUCE.

SNAPSHOTS

/

A SNAPSHOT BECOMES PHOTOVIZ WHEN IT CAN EXPRESS INFORMATION ABOUT THE DEPICTED SCENE THAT IS NOT TYPICALLY VISIBLE OR NATURALLY APPARENT. DEVICES LIKE THE MICROSCOPE OR TELESCOPE AND TECHNIQUES LIKE X-RAY OR MRI ARE ABLE TO CAPTURE THE INVISIBLE, BUT CAPTURE ONLY A SINGLE VIEW. BY COMBINING MULTIPLE MOMENTS OR PERSPECTIVES, PHOTOVIZ SNAPSHOTS ARE DISTINGUISHED BY THE COMPARISONS THEY ALLOW AND THE LARGER VIEW THEY CREATE.

TRACES: WHEN A MALLEABLE MATERIAL LIKE SNOW OR PAINT IS INTRODUCED INTO AN ENVIRONMENT, ITS SURFACE BECOMES SENSITIZED TO ACTIVITY LIKE A PIECE OF FILM OR PHOTOGRAPHIC PAPER. THIS "EMULSION"

7.
BABAK FAKHAMZADEH
Once Salone
see pp. 184–187

8.
GARY SETTLES
Schlieren Photography
see pp. 66–67

CAN RECORD PROCESSES OVER TIME AND REVEAL AGGREGATE BEHAVIORS. SNOW ON THE SIDEWALK OR PAINT ON A STREET ARE ALTERED AND DEGRADED BY THE ACTIONS OF PEOPLE AND CARS. THESE ACTIVITIES COMPOUND TO REVEAL PRIOR MOVEMENTS ON THEIR SURFACE, EVEN AS THE PHOTO SIMPLY CAPTURES A SINGLE MOMENT IN TIME.[6]

THEN & NOW: RE-FRAMING AN OLD PHOTO IN A CONTEMPORARY CONTEXT CREATES A LINK THAT ENABLES COMPARISON AND A CONNECTION BETWEEN THESE TWO MOMENTS. THIS SIMPLE LAYERING ALLOWS A SNAPSHOT TO EXPRESS A MUCH LONGER STORY BY REVEALING THE FORGOTTEN HISTORY OF A PLACE.[7]

SCHLIEREN PHOTOGRAPHY: **AN OPTICAL PROCESS KNOWN AS A SCHLIEREN SYSTEM REVEALS THE FLOW OF FLUIDS WITH VARYING DENSITIES IN PLAIN SIGHT. WITH A BRIGHT LIGHT, A CURVED MIRROR, LENSES, AND A KNIFE EDGE, DISTURBANCES AND TEMPERATURE CHANGES IN AIR CAN BE MADE VISIBLE. BY COMBINING THE SCHLIEREN TECHNIQUE WITH HIGH SPEED PHOTOGRAPHY, THE SHOCK WAVES MADE BY THE FIRING OF A RIFLE OR THE PLUME OF AIR PRODUCED BY A COUGH CAN BE REVEALED.**[8]

6.
HERBERT LIST
Footprints in the Snow/
Letzter Schnee

EXPOSURES

/

BY MANIPULATING THE WAY AN IMAGE IS CAPTURED, SEVERAL PHOTOVIZ TECHNIQUES CAN BE ACHIEVED WITHOUT USING POST-PROCESSING. THESE APPROACHES EXPAND OUR PERCEPTION BY RE-FRAMING TIME OR PRESENTING A DIFFERENT FIELD OF VIEW.

LONG-EXPOSURE: AT AROUND 1/30TH OF A SECOND, THE BRAIN BEGINS TO PERCEIVE THE FRAMES OF AN ANIMATION AS A SMOOTHLY MOVING IMAGE AN OPTICAL ILLUSION KNOWN AS THE PHI PHENOMENON. ONCE THE SHUTTER SPEED OF A CAMERA EXCEEDS

10.
ÉTIENNE-JULES MAREY
Chronophotographic Gun

THIS LIMIT, PHOTOGRAPHY BEGINS TO REVEAL PHENOMENA THAT ARE TYPICALLY IMPERCEPTIBLE. USING SHUTTER SPEEDS RANGING FROM MINUTES TO YEARS, LONG-EXPOSURE PHOTOGRAPHY CAN REVEAL THE BLUR OF A PASSING CROWD, THE CONSTRUCTION OF A BUILDING, OR THE MOVEMENT OF STARS.[9]

MULTIPLE-EXPOSURE: IN 1882, ETIENNE-JULES MAREY DEVELOPED HIS CHRONOPHOTOGRAPHIC GUN, A CAMERA CAPABLE OF SHOOTING 12 FRAMES PER SECOND ON A SINGLE NEGATIVE.[10] WITH THIS "GUN" HE WAS ABLE TO DECONSTRUCT THE MOTION OF A VARIETY OF ANIMALS AS WELL AS COMPLEX HUMAN MOVEMENTS LIKE RUNNING AND JUMPING. THESE EARLY MULTIPLE-EXPOSURE PHOTOGRAPHS INSPIRED A GENERATION OF 1950S PHOTOGRAPHERS LIKE HAROLD E. EDGERTON AND GJON MILI WHO PIONEERED THE USE OF STROBE LIGHTING TO FREEZE TIME FOR SINGLE AND MULTIPLE EXPOSURES.[11] WHILE EDGERTON FAMOUSLY FROZE MILK DROPS AND THE FLIGHT OF BULLETS, MILI DISSECTED EVERY MOVEMENT HE COULD FIND, FROM BALLERINAS TO MUSICIANS TO ATHLETES. ESSENTIALLY, THIS APPROACH

9.
MICHAEL WESELY
New Urban Fabric
see pp. 198–199

PRODUCES A PHOTOGRAPHIC DIAGRAM OF THE PRE-CISE MOVEMENTS OF AN OBJECT THROUGH TIME AND CONTINUES TO BE A STRIKING MEANS OF VISUALIZING MOTION TODAY.

SLIT SCAN: THE SLIT SCAN TECHNIQUE WAS WIDE-LY USED FOR CAPTURING PANORAMIC PHOTOS IN THE PAST. A CAMERA WITH A THIN VERTICAL APER-TURE ROTATES WHILE THE FILM IS ADVANCED SLOW-LY AND EXPOSED, SLICE BY SLICE. IF THE APERTURE IS STATIC RELATIVE TO THE SCENE, THE FILM WILL BE CONTINUOUSLY EXPOSED, YIELDING AN EXTRUDED SMEAR OF COLORS. ANY OBJECT PASSING THROUGH THIS THIN FIELD OF VIEW IS CAPTURED ONE SLICE AT A TIME AGAINST THE EXTRUDED LINES OF THE BACK-GROUND. IN EFFECT, SLIT SCAN PHOTOGRAPHY ISO-LATES MOVING OBJECTS, ACHIEVING THE OPPOSITE OF LONG-EXPOSURE PHOTOGRAPHY WHICH OFTEN RE-MOVES TRACES OF MOVING OBJECTS.

PANORAMA: PANORAMIC IMAGES PRODUCED BY MOVING THE CAMERA RESULT IN A PHOTOGRAPH WHERE DIFFERENT SECTIONS OF THE IMAGE OC-CURRED AT DIFFERENT TIMES. AN EXPOSURE MOVING THROUGH SPACE AND TIME MAKES THIS TECHNIQUE IDEAL FOR CAPTURING LONGER MOMENTS. DIGITAL CAMERAS AND SMART PHONES WITH PANORAMA FEA-TURES ARE CAPABLE OF CREATING SEAMLESS PHO-TOS BY DIGITALLY STITCHING TOGETHER A STREAM OF IMAGES AS THE PHONE IS PANNED. THIS FEATURE CAN BE RE-PURPOSED TO PRODUCE BEAUTIFUL COMPOS-ITES IF THE PHONE IS HELD STILL WHILE THE SCENE IS IN MOTION. INSTEAD OF STITCHING NEIGHBORING PHO-TOS INTO A PANORAMA, THE SOFTWARE IS FORCED TO STITCH MOMENTS AND COLLAPSE TIME. THIS ATTEMPT TO RECONCILE THE SOURCE IMAGES RENDERS MOTION VISIBLE BY EXTRUDING OR DUPLICATING OBJECTS IN MOTION LIKE PEOPLE OR VEHICLES.[12]

11.
GJON MILI
John Borican

12.
JIM HOUSER
see pp. 52-57

POST-PROCESSING

/

REORGANIZING AND RECOMBINING EXISTING PHOTOGRAPHS MAKES IT POSSIBLE TO CONDENSE IMAGES INTO A SINGLE INFORMATION-RICH AGGREGATE IMAGE. TECHNIQUES FOR POST-PROCESSING RANGE FROM HAND-MADE TO COMPUTER-ASSISTED AND FROM SUBTLE TO OVERT. THE COMPOSITE IMAGE CAN BE SO NUANCED THAT THE ALTERATION GOES UNNOTICED, OR IT CAN TRANSPORT THE SOURCE IMAGES SO FAR FROM THE ORIGINAL THAT ONLY THE VAGUEST CONNECTION REMAINS.

MOSAIC: A MOSAIC IS SIMULTANEOUSLY A SINGLE IMAGE AND MANY IMAGES. BY COMBINING MULTIPLE SMALL IMAGES IN A GRID, A SENSE OF THE AGGREGATE CAN EMERGE. FLUCTUATIONS IN COMPOSITION AND COLOR ALLOW COMMON TRAITS TO BECOME APPARENT AND OUTLIERS TO EMERGE (SEE "SHADOW BOXING THE WORLD," PP. 184–187).

14.
PETER FUNCH
Babel Tales
see pp. 104–111

STACKING: BY ALIGNING AND LAYERING MULTIPLE EXPOSURES OF THE SAME SCENE, SECTIONS OF THE PHOTOS CAN BE SELECTIVELY REVEALED TO DEMONSTRATE CHANGES OVER TIME. BY USING VERTICAL SLICES, THE CHANGE OF SEASONS OR THE TRANSITION FROM DAY TO NIGHT CAN BE VISUALIZED (SEE "REMAINS OF THE DAY," PP. 26–31). IN MORE FANCIFUL APPLICATIONS, DIFFERENT SHAPES, TRANSPARENCY, OR DIMENSIONS CAN BE INTRODUCED TO MERGE PHOTOS FROM DIFFERENT TIMES AND PERSPECTIVES WITH THE GOAL OF SHOWING THE SAME SUBJECT THROUGH DIFFERENT LENSES IN A SINGLE IMAGE.

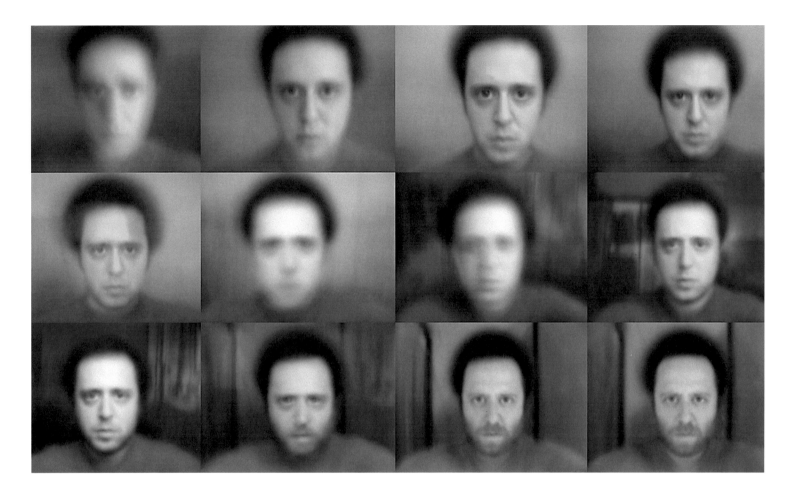

COLLAGE: **WHILE STACKED IMAGES MUST ALIGN TO SHOW THE SAME SCENE AT DIFFERENT TIMES, COLLAGE IS FREE TO REPOSITION IMAGES TO CREATE NEW SCENES AND NEW MEANING. IN THE MOST DECONSTRUCTED COMPOSITIONS, THE SAME ELEMENT MAY APPEAR SEVERAL TIMES TO CAPTURE BOTH MOVEMENT AND TIME, AS IN DAVID HOCKNEY'S WORK** (SEE "IN THE CUT," PP. 96-99).

AVERAGING: **AVERAGES CAN BE DECEPTIVE. THEY CAN BE HIGHLY REPRESENTATIVE OR ENTIRELY MISLEADING. BY ALIGNING AND BLENDING A SET OF IMAGES, A PHOTOGRAPHIC AVERAGE CAN BE PRODUCED THAT MAY BE REPRESENTATIVE OF THE SET OR MAY CREATE SOMETHING ENTIRELY NEW AND PREVIOUSLY UNAPPARENT IN THE COLLECTION.**[13]

BLEND: **WHILE GJON MILI'S EXPERIMENTS ALLOWED HIM TO SEAMLESSLY MERGE SEVERAL EXPOSURES INTO A SINGLE IMAGE, HE COULD NOT PHOTOGRAPH EVERYTHING. WITHOUT A DARK STUDIO OR A STROBE THOSE FAMOUS IMAGES WERE DIFFICULT TO RECREATE UNTIL THE DIGITAL ERA. MULTIPLE IMAGES CAN NOW BE STACKED AND COMBINED INTO A CONVINCING OR SURREAL COMPOSITE. SPORTS PHOTOGRAPHERS LOVE THE ABILITY TO BREAK DOWN INTRICATE MOVEMENTS INTO THEIR DISCRETE STEPS, WHILE ARTISTS HAVE DISCOVERED HOW SELECTIVE BLENDING ALLOWS THEM TO REORGANIZE THE WORLD.**[14]

DATA VIZ

/

A PHOTOGRAPH IS NOT ONLY AN IMAGE. IT IS ALSO A RESERVOIR OF INFORMATION. EXIF DATA ATTACHED TO DIGITAL IMAGES CAN STORE ATTRIBUTES INCLUDING THE TIME, LOCATION, ORIENTATION, APERTURE, SHUTTER SPEED AND THE CAMERA MODEL USED TO CREATE THE PHOTO. THE IMAGE ITSELF CAN BE FURTHER ANALYZED TO EXTRACT OBJECTS, BRANDS, EMOTIONS, PEOPLE, AND COLORS. WHEN SHARED, THE PHOTO MAY HAVE ADDITIONAL METADATA ATTACHED IN THE FORM OF PLACES, EMOJI, PEOPLE, OR HASHTAGS THAT ADD FURTHER CONTEXT.

ONCE THE LATENT INFORMATION IN A PHOTOGRAPH HAS BEEN CONVERTED TO DATA, IT CAN BE MANIPULATED AND VISUALIZED LIKE ANY OTHER DATA SET. PHOTOGRAPHS CAN BE SORTED, PLOTTED, MAPPED, FILTERED AND ORGANIZED BY ANY ATTRIBUTE. THIS "GOD'S EYE VIEW" OF PHOTOGRAPHY BECOMES INVALUABLE FOR AN INDIVIDUAL SEARCHING FOR THE RIGHT PHOTO AT THE RIGHT MOMENT, OR FOR GLOBAL UNDERSTANDING OF WORLD EVENTS DOCUMENTED THROUGH THOUSANDS—IF NOT MILLIONS—OF IMAGES.

METADATA VISUALIZATIONS: MOMENTS AND PLACES OF SIGNIFICANCE BEGIN TO EMERGE FROM LARGE IMAGE SETS WHEN VISUALIZING PHOTO METADATA. IN ERIC FISCHER'S VISUALIZATION OF FLICKR PHOTO LOCATIONS, THE POINTS OF INTEREST IN THE BAY AREA BECOME OBVIOUS WHEN MAPPED.[15] IN A VISUALIZATION OF THE TIMESTAMPS OF MY OWN PHOTOS, CLUSTERS OF IMPORTANCE APPEAR AND TRANSLATE DIRECTLY TO MEANINGFUL EVENTS AND TRAVEL.[16]

CONTENT VISUALIZATIONS: EXTRACTING AND VISUALIZING CONTENT FROM PHOTOS IS ONE OF THE MOST EXCITING AND RAPIDLY EVOLVING BRANCHES OF PHOTOVIZ. SIMPLE COMPUTATIONAL APPROACHES LIKE COLOR ANALYSIS AND MANUAL LOCATION AND PEOPLE TAGGING HAVE BEEN JOINED BY FACIAL RECOGNITION AND MACHINE LEARNING APPROACHES THAT CAN IDENTIFY PEOPLE, PLACES AND THINGS WITH UNPRECEDENTED SPEED AND SCALE.[17]

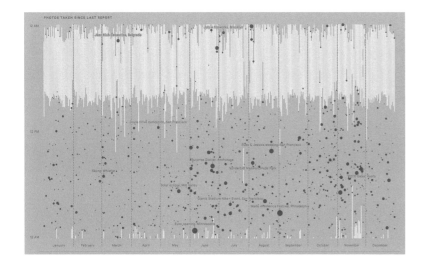

16.
NICHOLAS FELTON
2012 Annual Report

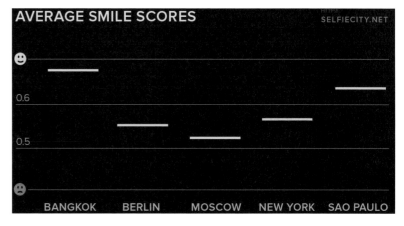

17.
LEV MANOVICH ET AL.
Selfiecity

15.
ERIC FISCHER
Locals and Tourists

CONCLUSION

I AM MESMERIZED BY THE IMAGES IN THIS BOOK. THEY REVEAL PATTERNS AND CONNECTIONS THAT CAN ARE FREQUENTLY INVISIBLE TO THE NAKED EYE. I AM ALSO ENAMORED WITH THE INGENUITY OF THE IMAGE MAKERS. THE BEAUTY OF THEIR ART IS ENOUGH TO DISTRACT FROM THE STRENGTH OF THE IDEAS THEY CONTAIN. WHILE TECHNOLOGICAL ADVANCEMENTS HAVE DRIVEN MUCH OF THE INNOVATION, THERE ARE ALSO REMINDERS THAT THE BEST SOLUTION TO A PROBLEM IS NOT ALWAYS MORE TECHNOLOGY. FEW PEOPLE WOULD IMAGINE THAT THE BEST WAY TO VISUALIZE THE RADIO FIELD OF AN RFID-CHIP WOULD BE THROUGH LONG-EXPOSURE PHOTOGRAPHY.[18] BY SHARING THESE PROJECTS I HOPE TO SEE GREATER APPLICATIONS AND FURTHER EVOLUTION OF THESE APPROACHES. THE BOUNDARIES OF PHOTOVIZ ARE NOT FIXED, BUT I HOPE THAT ITS ASPIRATIONS AND IMPORTANCE ARE CLEAR.

APART FROM BEING ARTFUL AND INTERESTING, I SUSPECT THAT THESE TECHNIQUES AND THEIR DESCENDANTS WILL BECOME INVALUABLE. THE PHRASE "PICS OR IT DIDN'T HAPPEN" WAS ONCE NOVEL BUT IS NOW A SIMPLE TRUISM. THE FAMILY PHOTOGRAPHER HAS BECOME EVERYONE AND WILL SOON BE EVERYTHING. THERE IS SIMPLY NO LIMIT TO HOW MUCH PHOTOGRAPHY WE WILL PRODUCE, AND WITHOUT TECHNIQUES TO MANAGE, UNDERSTAND, AND CONSOLIDATE THE PHOTOGRAPHIC FUTURE, OUR IMAGES WILL GO UNSEEN.

18.
TIMO ARNALL
Immaterials: Ghost in the Field

WHAT THE FUTURE HOLDS

/

Technology creates tools whose uses we must first discover. So does art. New approaches and aesthetics may exist for years, as novelties or possibilities, before their full range of applications are uncovered and explored. Like gunpowder, which was used to make fireworks before it was employed to topple castles or to pave the way to rocketry and spaceflight. This book explores new technologies and new applications of established aesthetic techniques that possess equally explosive potential. For instance, drones have already opened the door to easily affordable

ONCE WE HAVE NEW TECHNIQUES AND NEW AESTHETICS, WE MUST EXPLORE THEM.

aerial photography, but photographers and artists are only just beginning to explore their potential. Light field photography may allow photographers to shoot first and focus later. Meanwhile, the wide availability of HD video and cheap storage is changing what it means to take a photograph even as it challenges us to find new ways to process and display the steadily increasing number of images we record. These advances will also drive changes in the ways we interact with and experience photographs in our own lives. They will heighten visual literacy and leave us better equipped than ever to find and create meaning in photography.

While some technologies may arrive with obvious photographic applications, many or even all of them only hint at their true potential as tools for visualizing and analyzing information and narratives. Consider the evolution of light paintings from aesthetic novelties to sci-fi photographic visualization tools (an evolution that plays out in the pages that follow). The technique—combining long exposures with a deliberately moved light source—has existed at least since the 1940s, when Gjon Mili and Picasso used it to make sketches in the air at the latter's studio (pp. 240–241). Recently, photographers have begun using it in more powerful ways. For instance, Arnall, Knutsen, and Martinussen's *Immaterials: Light Painting WiFi* (pp. 244–245) uses light painting to reveal the invisible terrain of Wi-Fi networks in our cities. The team paired the old technique with new Wi-Fi signal detectors. The results are a long way from Picasso's air-drawings: they help us to visualize information about our networked world, on location and without resorting to computer graphics. Once we have new techniques and new aesthetics, we must explore them.

DRONE ART AND EXPENDABLE PHOTOGRAPHERS.

Drones with mounted cameras have already become useful tools for photography, yet they can be used for more than just straightforward aerial footage. Martin Kimbell's *Transient Light* series (facing page and pp. 236–239) uses them for a kind of light painting, but as the previous examples demonstrate, such aesthetic experiments are only the beginning of what may be possible in the field of photographic visualization. For instance: what would be possible if drones were used to illuminate the scene of a long-exposure photograph rather than for light paintings? They could selectively light or "paint" a path that a figure is following (or should have been following). Or highlight different parts of the scene at different times. They could be used for multiple-exposure or stroboscopic photographs wherein the light source—or even the drone-mounted camera—actively moves around the subject, lighting up different areas or angles as the motion progresses. Or for new kinds of panoramic photographs, like Aydın Büyüktaş's recent *Flatlands* series »

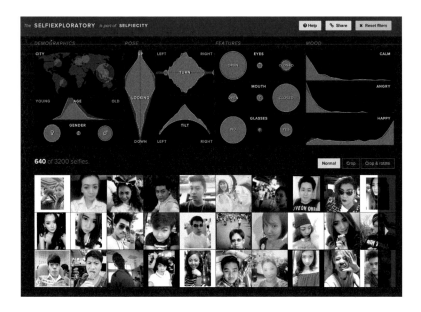

of folded aerial shots. Or for purposes that we have not even begun to consider yet. And since they are relatively inexpensive and capable of transmitting their photos or videos back to the photographer, or even to the cloud, they are expendable. That means they can be sent into risky situations or even sacrificed for the sake of a shot. Each new use of drones is only the beginning of a whole range of possibilities, because those new applications can then be combined with all the other techniques presented in this book to create even more aesthetic and photographic visualization methods.

SHOOT FIRST, FOCUS LATER.

New photographic technology may change the way that we take photographs, which may in turn change how we approach photographic visualization. For instance, light field photography is filtering down to consumer availability. Light field or plenoptic cameras capture information about the intensity of light in a scene, as well as information about the direction that the light rays are traveling in space. They record more of the source conditions. The technique makes it possible to make changes after the fact—for instance, it is possible to adjust the focus after the picture has been taken. That means that future cameras may simply capture masses of data about a scene that can be edited later. Cartier-Bresson's decisive mo-

ment would take on a new significance, as photographers would be more free to move and observe, seeking that moment without having to worry about lighting, exposure, focus, etc., because those details can be addressed afterwards without degrading the image. Combined with post-processing techniques like compositing, blending, averaging, etc., technologies like light field photography will result in new and unexpected avenues for photographic visualization to explore.

FROM LONG EXPOSURE TO CONTINUOUS EXPOSURE.

There is also the issue of video. Now that cheap, ubiquitous, always-available HD video is becoming a reality, it is possible to tap into streams of photos that are not only constant but also seamless. Any frame or frames of a HD video can be repurposed as a photograph. Some of these photo and video streams flow from individuals intentionally documenting their lives and hobbies, but others are the passive products of surveillance, like private or semi-private CCTV footage, or recordings produced for services or research, like Google Street View. There are so many streams that people sometimes hijack them for their own purposes, like guerilla drama groups that stage surveillance camera theater, or people who enact scenes meant to be recorded by passing Street View cars.

WE CAN TAP INTO STREAMS OF PHOTOS THAT ARE NOT ONLY CONSTANT BUT ALSO SEAMLESS.

Coping with the flood of images will require new tools. The way that we experience photographs may be mediated by algorithms that not only sort and select images that are relevant to our needs, but that also actively shape their content. Facebook can already detect users' faces in photos uploaded to its servers, Google Image Search allows users to sort results by color, and the photosharing startup EyeEm recently produced a

DATA MAY BECOME ART, WHICH MAY THEN BECOME A NEW WAY OF VISUALIZING INFORMATION AND NARRATIVES.

computer vision engine, EyeEm Vision, that can tag photographs based on their content. The latter is pushing the boundaries even further with an "aesthetic algorithm" that can identify "good" photographs.

Computers will play an increasing role in determining what photographs we see. They may also determine how we see them. For instance, automated software like RapidRecap produces brief video synopses of several hours of footage, which can also be compressed into composite photographs. It selects the relevant moments to show to busy users. But there is still room for creative human intervention. For instance, Lev Manovich's *On Broadway* and *Selfiecity* projects (see facing page) present hybrid data/photo visualizations of sets of photographs as well as their content. On a less data-driven level, Cy Kuckenbaker has produced his own versions of video-derived composite images (pp. 112–115). The results are similar to an automatic composite, yet they show the potential for an artist to shape such images in order to tell stories. And they are only the beginning. Data may become art, which may then become a new way of visualizing information and narratives. Beyond composites, techniques like averaging could be employed or combined to make sense of the wealth of images that big photo offers.

NEW WAYS OF LOOKING AT PHOTOGRAPHS.

As we spend more and more time online, and screens and monitors become increasingly ubiquitous, photographs no longer need to be static. Animated GIFs can be created from video clips, but they can also be created from any set of still images—including images that have already undergone other photographic visualization treatments. As the photographer Fong Qi Wei notes (pp. 26–31), we experience a scene not as a snapshot—a single moment—but as a series of moments. Many photographic visualization techniques attempt to capture a span of time or a movement and then to dramatize it in a static image. But an animated GIF already does that just by its nature, creating little loops of action, from minute changes to radical transformations. This opens up new terrain, not only as a technique in itself, but also as a new way to layer and combine other techniques: imagine ghostly long-exposure photographs looped together, or composite photographs that reveal what was added or subtracted from the frame. And since animated GIFs are just special instances of the GIF file format, which is also used for sharing still images, they can also be embedded in documents or websites (or digital picture frames) like normal photographs. They are narrative micro bundles that bridge the gap between stills and videos but that are still shareable as single images.

AND THEN THERE'S THE HUMAN FACTOR.

The preceding examples are largely concerned with the effects of technology on producing and presenting photography, but there is also the question of how it affects the way that we actually experience and perceive it. Part of the power of photography as a tool for visualization lies in the audience understanding how something was or could be visualized. It is a question of growing visual

AS TECHNOLOGY MAKES IT EASIER TO MAKE AND SHARE PHOTOS, IT WILL ALSO INCREASE VISUAL LITERACY.

literacy. Thanks to smartphones and photosharing, more of us than ever before are thinking about photography and the ways it presents information or tells stories—just look at selfies and the wealth of signs and symbols they contain.   »

As technology makes it easier to make and share photos, it will increase visual literacy as a side effect. But there are other technologies that have the potential to actively increase visual literacy, like EyeEm's Open Edit, which allows users to see how photographs have been edited. Users can see how parameters like sharpness and contrast, etc., were changed with the tap of a button. On the one hand, it or something like it could grow to become a tool for learning how to produce better photographs or for tutoring users in how to apply photographic visualization techniques by showing real-world applications, step by step. But it could also be used to increase skepticism about the manipulations that lie at the heart of many photographs. Similar tools could strip back the layers of composite photographs, showing what was originally there and what was added, or revealing just how much an image of a model has been photoshopped to create an unattainable ideal. All of this will create a feedback loop—the more conscious people are of aesthetic and technological techniques, the more able they will be to find ways to use them, and vice versa.

PHOTOGRAPHY UNBOUND.

As Nicholas Felton notes, advances in technology will remove the limits on how much photography we will produce and will challenge us to find ways to manage and understand the resulting ocean of images. But those advances will also remove the limits on how we produce photography and how we interact with and perceive it. Despite touching on science fiction, these advances all rest within the larger photographic tradition and build on or coexist with established techniques, like long exposures or collages. Rather than replacing older techniques, the new ones will only make them more powerful. Some of the projects featured in this book are clear examples of photographic visualization in action—others are the first bright fireworks sent up into the night sky in the hope of inspiring future photographers or technologists to find new uses for them. Thanks to new technology and the techniques presented in the following pages, we are now better equipped than ever to visualize information about our world and to tell stories about our lives.

ERIC FISCHER
See Something or Say Something

CLOCKWORKS

Combining sequential photos
of a single location to illustrate
the passage of day to night

TIME SLICE GLOBAL_
RICHARD SILVER

This series uses a collage technique to document the passage of time. Each photo is an assemblage of a selection of 36 photographs taken before, during, and after sunset. Slices were cut from each photograph and ordered from day to night running left to right. Each image has a horizontal axis representing the passage of time, which is made visible by changes in the light. Those changes also reflect the motion of the sun along an unseen vertical axis. The resulting stripes invite the viewer to examine the images more closely and mark them as something more than typical photographs of landmarks.

REMAINS OF THE DAY

Digital composites of photographs
from different times of day

TIME IS A DIMENSION_
FONG QI WEI

Photographer Fong Qi Wei writes that "our experience of a scene is more than a snap-shot"—not a single frame but a sequence of events. By creating panels and concentric layers out of landscapes, cityscapes, and seascapes photographed several times over a span of two to four hours, he was able to assemble images that seem to ripple with light and activity even though they are largely static scenes. The subject of the photos is the experience of time. By playing with the size and angle of the panels and inserting some out of order, he succeeds in dramatizing the normally gradual and almost imperceptible transition from day to night.

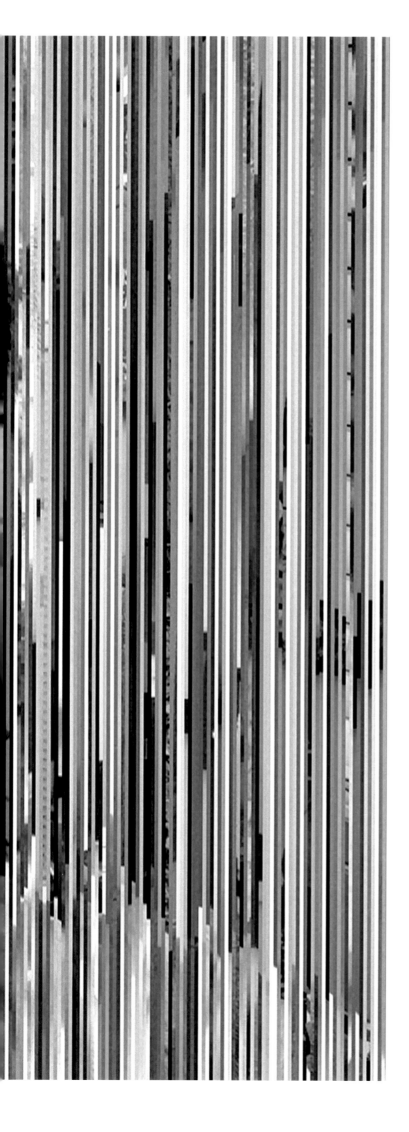

365 DEGREES

A full year of daily self-portraits sliced into ribbons and reassembled into a single image to document the shifting nature of identity and the passage of time

Where a self-portrait is a representation of identity, this series is a representation of the self as it changes over time. By loading a full year of photographs into Photoshop and then slicing them with guides, Dylan Mason was able to create an axis representing the flow of time (left to right, January 1 through December 31). The results resemble the growth rings of a tree trunk, yet it is difficult to determine how that growth is progressing. The many bands of color and the way that an image distorts while still being recognizable emphasize how much we can vary from day to day while still retaining our identities.

EVERYDAY_
DYLAN MASON

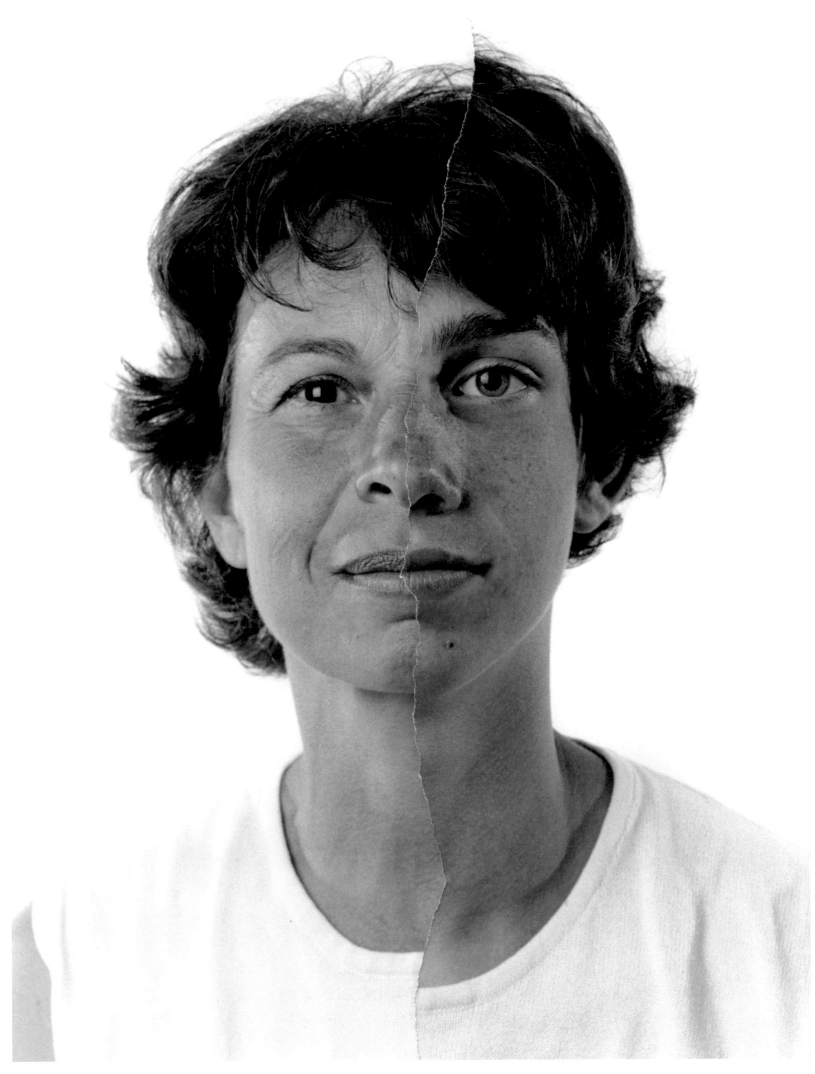

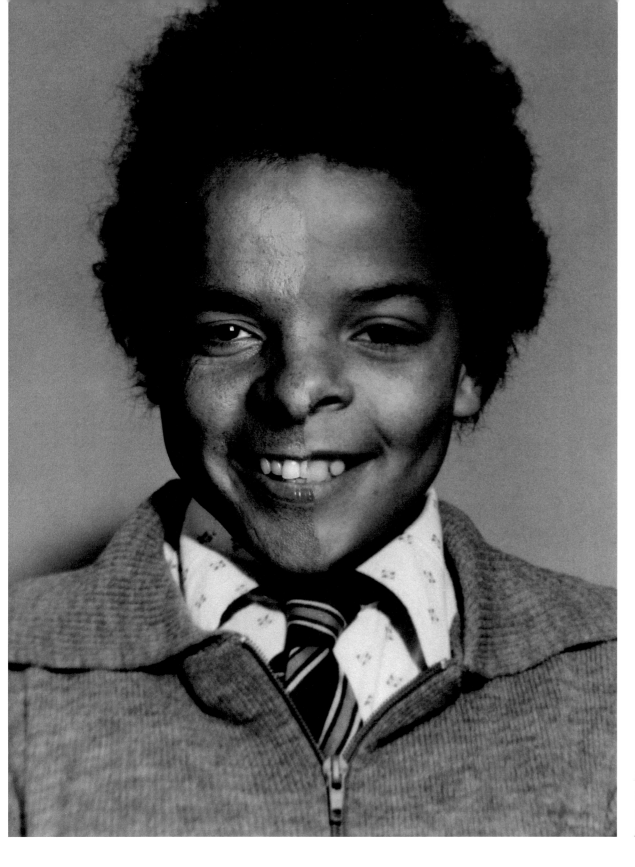

WHEN I GROW UP

The passage of time and family
relationships documented by
tearing and recombining photos

Eschewing digital manipulation, Bobby Neel Adams uses what he calls
photo-surgery to create these two-piece collages. Two photos of each subject in the same pose are scaled and printed, and then carefully torn and
reassembled. The tears add an interesting organic, physical element to the
resulting images, which sets them apart from other before/after visualizations. The technique can matter as much as the artist's intent, since a
visualization is not just a means of transmitting data but also an aesthetic
product. Had Adams simply split the paired images in half down the middle
using Photoshop, the results would be far less engaging.

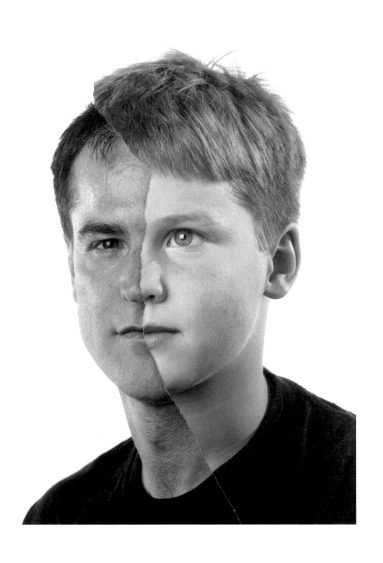

BOBBY NEEL ADAMS

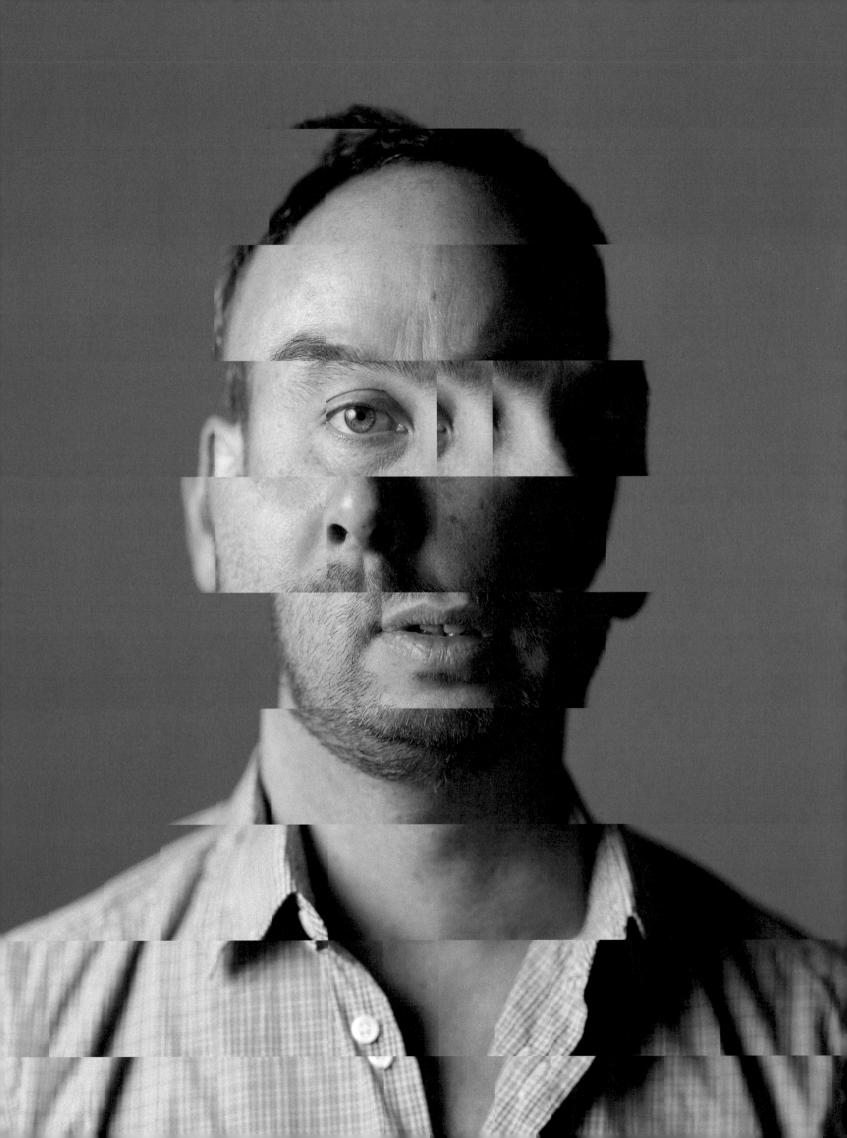

UNLOCKING THE DOOR TO MY OWN SELF

Twenty-minute portraits taken by a camera
travelling along a fixed path around the subject

PORTRAITS AND
STATIC NO. 12_
DANIEL CROOKS

DANIEL CROOKS

STATIC NO. 12

These portraits were achieved by combining many separate photographs taken over the course of 20 minutes. Not only time but also space varies between each fragment, as the camera was mounted on a robot that followed a fixed path around the subject. The results are fragmentary shots of the subjects taken from several vantage points at once. *Static No. 12* adopts a different approach. It is a still from a video depicting an old man performing tai chi. The video was produced using slit-scan photography, which causes the static background to become a blur of motion while sending the meditating man swirling across time and space.

COME FULL CIRCLE

A surfer backflips over a wave, the individual stages captured in a composite photograph

A wave arcs, curls, and crashes as a lone surfer describes a windblown parabola over the water. Agustin Muñoz captured the event in a series of quick shots and composited them into a single frame. The post-processing is evident in the way that the images of the surfer are ordered. Chronologically, the flip begins on the right and ends on the left. But if the images had been overlaid in the order they were taken, the image to the left would always obscure the image to the right. Instead, the images are layered in the opposite order—a deliberate choice that yields a better view of the surfer while inviting us to imagine the flip in reverse.

SEQUENCES_
AGUSTIN MUÑOZ

SWARM INTELLIGENCE

Images made by digitally tracing the paths
of flying birds in video footage

VISUALIZATIONS
OF THE FLIGHT
PATHS OF BIRDS_
DENNIS HLYNSKY

Flying birds become windblown streamers or curling dragons when their flight paths are made visible. The choreography of flocking becomes a ribbon dance as groups synchronize and individuals add their own flourishes. The images are both revelatory documents and mysterious artefacts that seem to show our everyday world in an unnatural light. Dennis Hlynsky began with videos of birds and then digitally traced the paths they followed. That video data could then be converted into composite images capturing seconds or minutes of flight in a single frame. They represent photographic visualization "at the intersection of art and science."

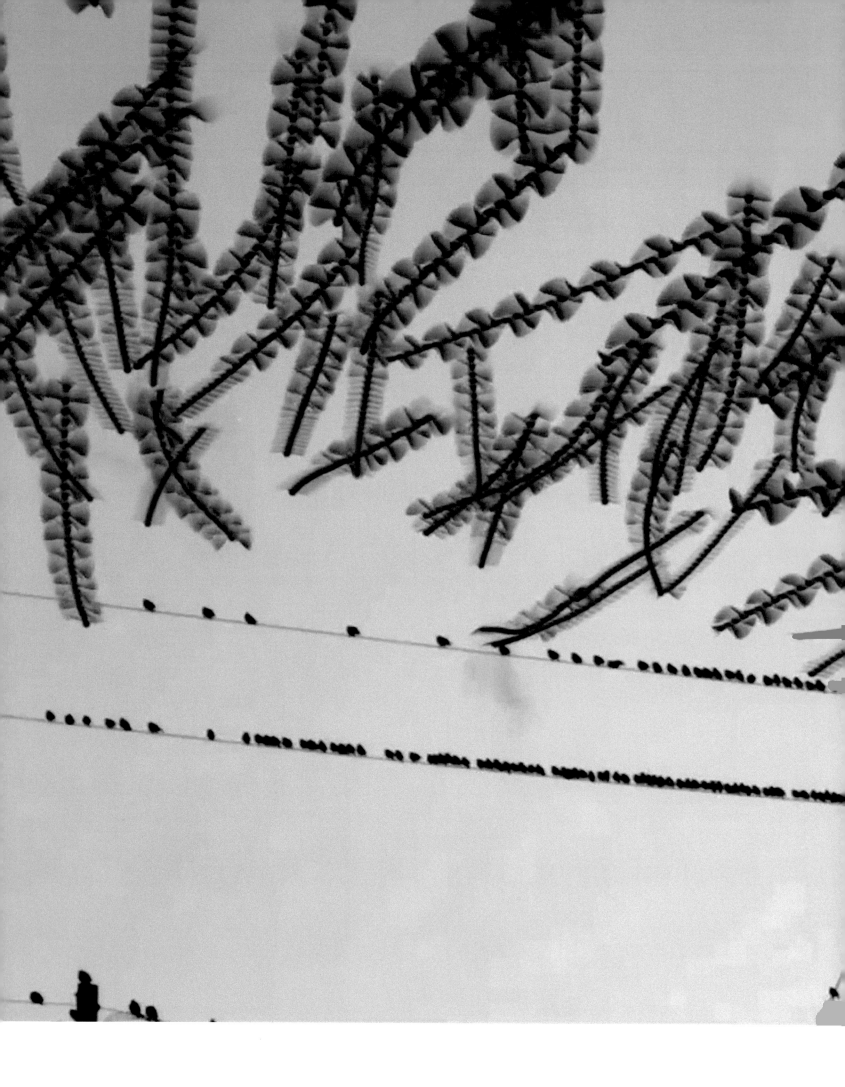

VISUALIZATIONS OF THE FLIGHT PATHS OF BIRDS

WORM THEORY

Panoramic photographs taken without moving the camera

This series began as happy accidents resulting from experiments with new technology (the iPhone camera's panorama feature) and the attempts of a father to capture "a little boy who could never stay still." Rather than moving the camera to capture slices of a wider view that the software would then stitch together into a long horizontal image, the camera was held steady and sequential images were stitched together in the same frame. They are not panoramas of space but of time. The stitching algorithm creates glitches, fragmenting the bodies in motion. The technique shows the power of chance and the potential hidden in each camera.

—

J I M   H O U S E R

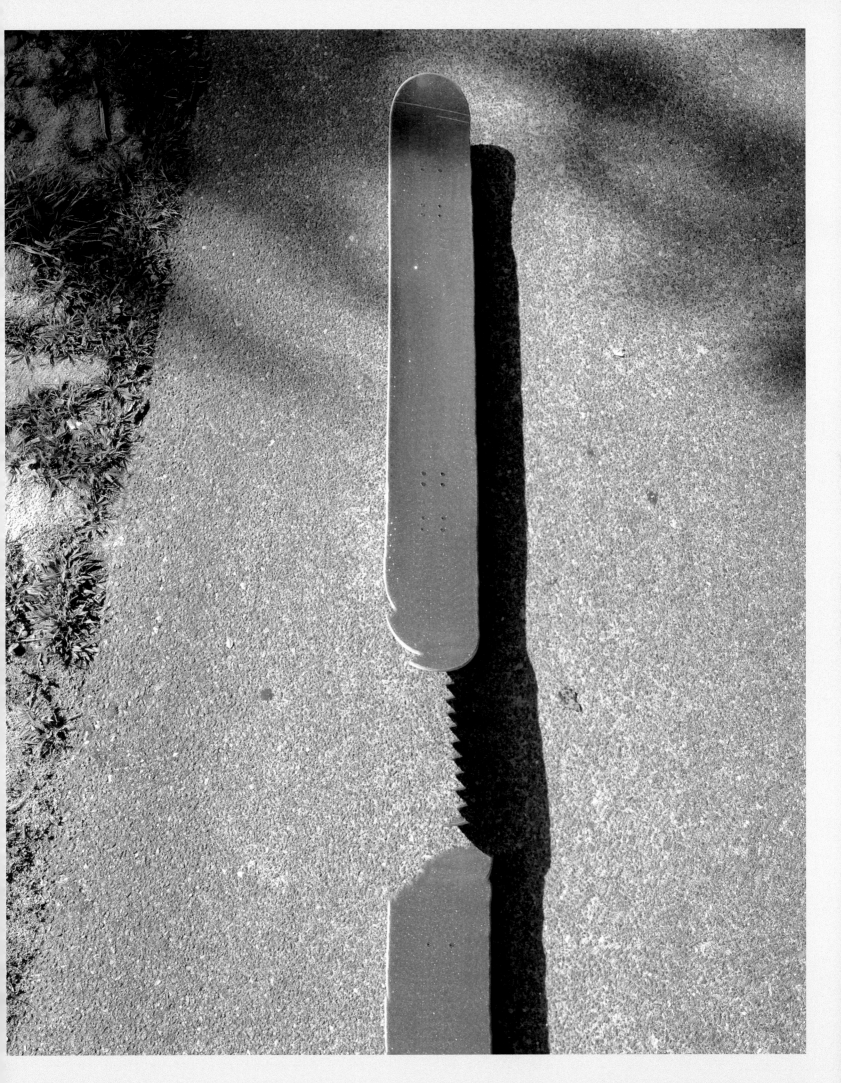

JIM HOUSER

CONSTANTS & VARIABLES

A refinement of multiple-exposure
photography with control over the timing
and number of flashes

CHRONOPHOTO_
JEAN-YVES LEMOIGNE

Paying tribute to and expanding on the work of stroboscopic photography pioneers like Gjon Mili and photographic researchers like Eadweard Muybridge, who explored human movement, Jean-Yves Lemoigne's series uses strobe lights and long exposures to capture the motions of tennis players. The effect is still achieved in-camera, but the use of modern technology makes it possible to control the timing between flashes and the number of flashes more precisely, giving the photographer a degree of control over how the movement will be portrayed in each photograph. While time is an element of each photo, there is no axis: all moments exist at the same time.

MULTIPLE SUNS

An analemma shows the position of the sun at one location and time of day throughout the year

A camera situated at the Milchsuppenstein in Zug took a series of photographs from the same position and angle and at the same time of day for a year. The resulting image presents an array of multiple suns in an elongated figure-eight arrangement known as an analemma. The distortion of the figure eight reflects the tilt of the Earth's axis and the variation in its orbit. By tracking the changing position of the sun in the sky, *Analemma for Kunsthaus Zug* makes the movement of the earth over the course of a year explicit and demonstrates the power of photography to reveal unseen patterns in nature.

ANALEMMA FOR
KUNSTHAUS ZUG_
OLAFUR ELIASSON

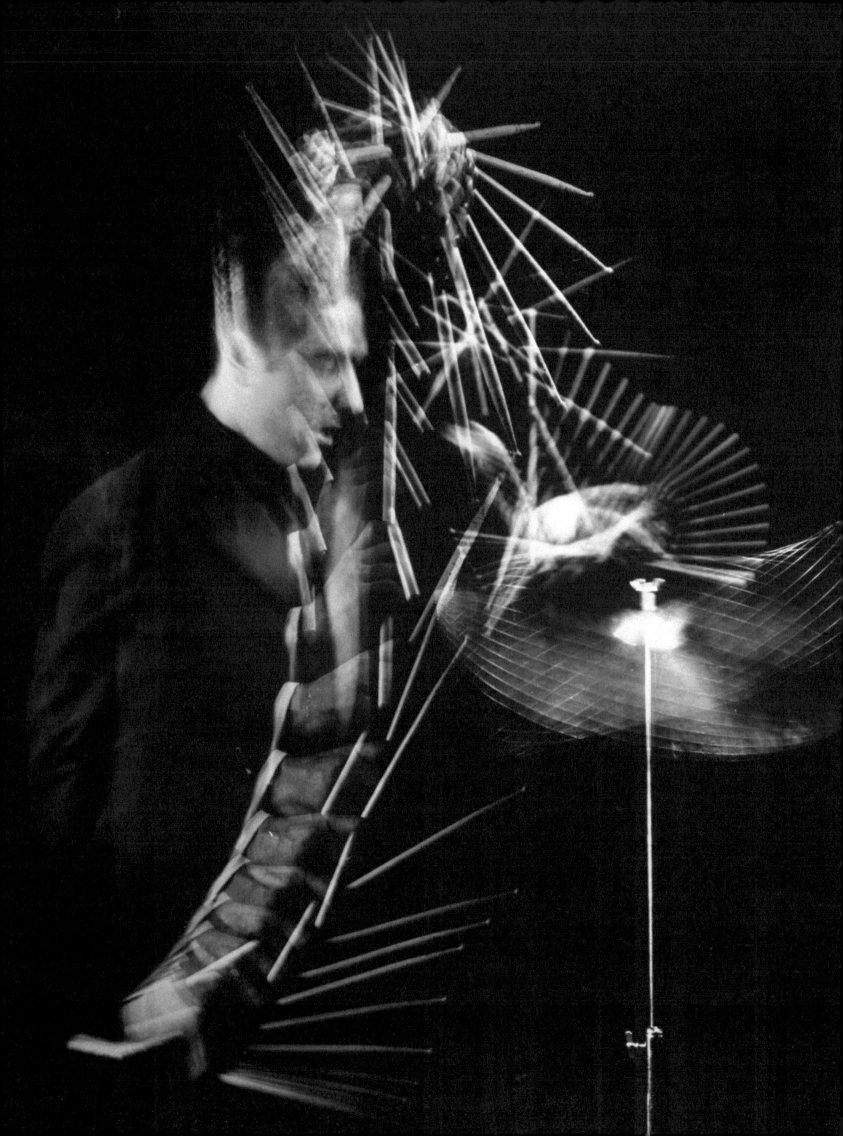

KEEPING TIME

Stroboscopic photography captures
the rhythm of 1941 on film

    A stroboscope emits rapid, periodic flashes of light that isolate individual moments in time. If life is a film, a strobe light enables you to see the individual frames. Combined with a camera, a strobe light enables you to capture those individual frames within a single photo. Where a long-exposure photograph blurs an action into an indistinct image, a stroboscopic photograph sharpens that action into a series of distinct moments. It is a form of multiple-exposure photography. Gjon Mili pioneered the use of stroboscopes in the 1940s to artfully capture the flow of movement, as seen in his photographs of a drummer playing his kit.

STROBOSCOPIC
PHOTOS_
GJON MILI

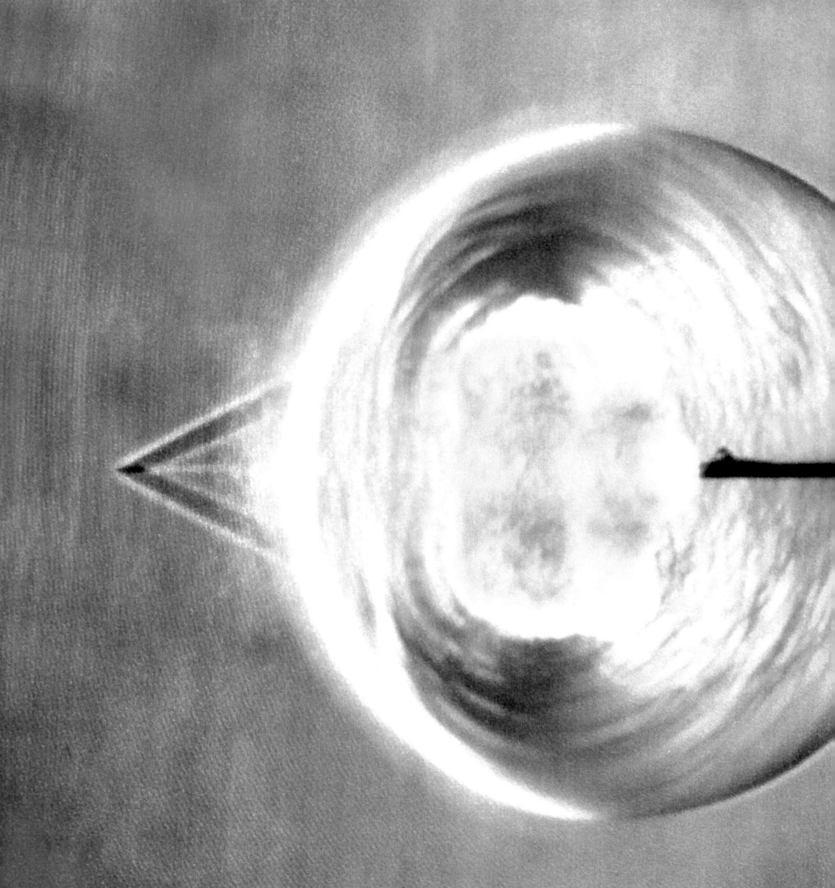

Not every visualization requires a long exposure or post-processing. In this case, the exposure lasted a mere four microseconds, capturing a supersonic bullet emerging from the spherical muzzle blast of a high-powered .30–06 rifle. To document the blast and the air displaced by the speeding bullet, a schlieren optical system with a curved mirror was employed.

Schlieren photography can detect the movement of fluids or gasses, even ones that we cannot see. Such images reveal how we constantly interact with the atmosphere on a physical level— we are immersed in it and do not really perceive it, but a photograph can make it visible.

FLUID DYNAMICS

Schlieren photography captures the muzzle blast of a rifle

GARY S. SETTLES

Layering of selected photographs in post-production to create single-frame choreographies

Composition, choreography, staging, and layering can be powerful tools in photo visualization. By way of such techniques, the photographer can choose which moments of time or details of movement will be preserved or highlighted. Though Nir Arieli's project is visually similar to long-exposure or strobe photos, they are made of deliberately selected images rather than continuous exposures. Taking photographs as the dancers danced, Arieli layered the images afterwards in order to present his own interpretation of the choreography. This approach allows the artist to benefit from interesting coincidences while still being able to edit the results.

O BODY SWAYED TO MUSIC

TENSION_
NIR ARIELI

WHEN TWO
BECOME NONE

The act of intercourse
as recorded in a single
long-exposure photograph

INTERNET/SEX_
NOAH KALINA

This series documents sexual intercourse, which appears both as an act of union between two individuals and as the dissolution of the self. Each image records the complete act in a single frame. In the images, not only do the two individuals merge into a single indistinct form, but that new form is itself often no longer recognizable for what it is. The background shows through. Perhaps physically, as well as mentally, the couple is in another place. Rather than documenting the physical reality of the act, like the positions or motion, Noah Kalina uses long exposures to document an unseen emotional reality.

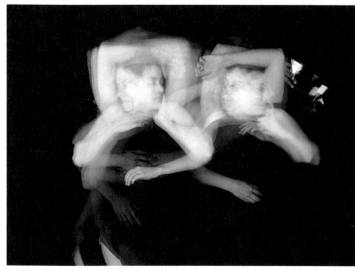

THE SLEEP OF THE
BELOVED_
**PAUL MARIA
SCHNEGGENBURGER**

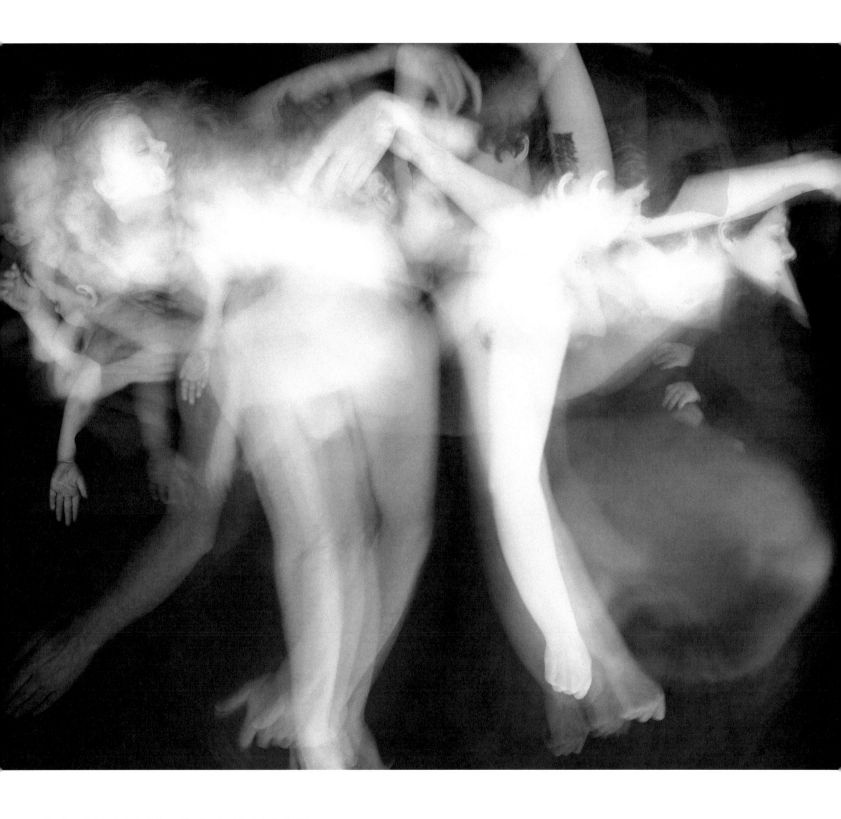

SLEEPWALTZING

All-night exposures reveal the dreamlike
ballet of people as they sleep

This series depicts people sleeping over the course of a night, capturing both their physical, spatial relationships with each other and creating a visual representation of their emotional relationships as well. Especially at this time scale (six hours), long-exposure photography tends to blur the subject—and yet in this case, distinct features, poses, or even scenes emerge like moments from a half-remembered dream. Photographer Paul Maria Schneggenburger was not present while the photographs were being exposed—the images are the result of a combination of his careful preparations and beautiful coincidences.

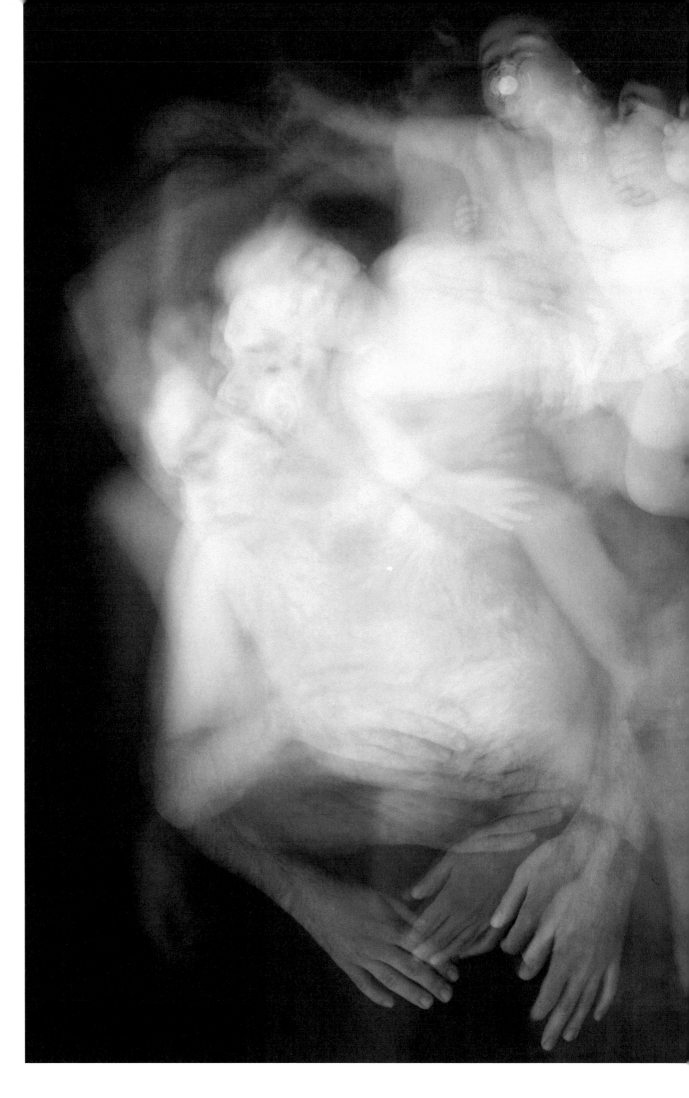

Color printing is essential to this photo visualization. It depicts the photographer's father over the course of four moments captured in four separate photographs, each of which was then filtered and printed in just one color. The resulting image appears at first glance to be a normal photograph with a colorful abstract effect near the subject's arm. But a closer look reveals that the solid, static, black-and-white parts of the photo are the result of the layering of the four CMYK prints, while the colors are the result of the lack of layering because of the different positions of the arm as it moved.

MUNITIONSFABRIK 17_
PIERO GLINA,
MARTIN BORST

AFTER IMAGES

An act of movement transformed into a process of printing: four photographs, each printed as a single CMYK channel, perceived by our eyes as a single image

THE COLOR OF TIME

A Harris shutter exposes the same frame three times, applying red, green, and blue filters in turn

The Harris shutter, which refers to both a device and a related (now digital) technique, is a means of making three exposures of a single frame of film, one for each primary color. If there is no motion in the frame, then the photograph will appear normal: the three colors can be combined to produce the full spectrum. However, anything that was in motion will stand out from the surroundings in separate red, green, and blue images. Because the order of the filters is fixed, it is possible to see not just the movement but also the flow of time: the earliest part of the movement will be red, the final moment will be blue.

TIRE SWING 5 &
HARRIS PLAYGROUND_
KEVIN L. FERGUSON

GHOSTS OF THE EVERYDAY

Long-exposure photographs of crowd scenes
reduce people to ghosts or clouds of smoke

CITY OF SHADOWS_
ALEXEY TITARENKO

In seeking to represent St. Petersburg in the years after the fall of Communism, Alexey Titarenko was concerned with documenting the atmosphere and emotional reality of the time. People seemed to him like phantasms from the underworld; wanting to find a visual metaphor that would enable the viewer to share his feelings as acutely as possible, he experimented with a long exposure process. The blurring that results from long exposures of moving objects caused the individuals in the crowds to dissolve into clouds or fade beneath ghostly flames. The images are not manipulated: they are just different views of reality through the lens.

ALEXEY TITARENKO

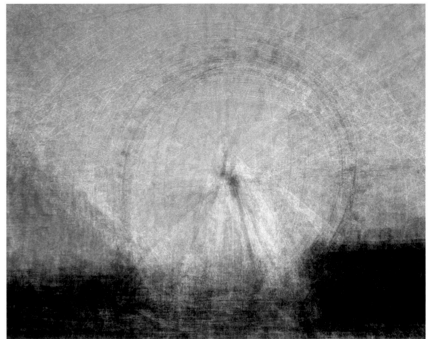

VISION OF THE CROWD

Digital composites of multitudes of photographs taken by tourists and averaged together to create impressionistic images of well-known attractions

Increasing the amount of data can lead to a decrease in the clarity of the image. In Bill Lytton's *London Tourism* series, hundreds of touristic photographs of popular locations and attractions are digitally averaged. The results resemble impressionistic paintings. Though in most cases the attractions remain recognizable, the specific details are often blurred away and only the rough forms remain. The images highlight the underlying dissimilarity of our shared experiences; we all see the same thing but never in quite the same way. Photographs seem to capture a sharp image of reality, but they are only ever impressions of the whole.

LONDON TOURISM _
BILL LYTTON

TRANSMETROPOLITAN

<u>Urban futures imagined by fusing panoramic</u>

<u>photographs taken from different angles</u>

NETROPOLIS_
MICHAEL NAJJAR

This series uses photographs of present-day metropolises to speculate about the way that cities will develop in the future. Michael Najjar traveled to 12 megacities and took panoramic photographs from high vantage points. Shooting from such perspectives transformed the massed buildings into landscapes. After photographing each city from several angles and locations, he combined them with digital post-processing to create densely interwoven images that depict a complex, highly networked urban future. The images could be mistaken for stills from a dystopian science fiction film, but they reflect what is happening in our world now.

FADING GREATNESS

Layered portraits of successive heads
of state from specific countries and periods

      Portraits are both the subject and the raw material of this series: Alejandro Almaraz layered between four and forty semi-transparent images of heads of state, both photographic and painted. Commonalities are emphasized in the solidity of the central image while artifacts like odd frames or ghostly halos emerge around them. Powerful figures sometimes disappear completely beneath images of lesser-known office holders. Each country appears to prefer a certain format, and similarities and differences in the way nations represent power are revealed. Here, photographic layering techniques also become a tool for creating abstract, painterly effects.

P O R T R A I T S   O F   P O W E R

ALEJANDRO ALMARAZ

The Crossword Puzzle Minniapolis Janu

IN THE CUT

Photographic collages
of snapshots arranged
to create images of larger
spaces or scenes

PHOTOGRAPHIC
COLLAGES_
DAVID HOCKNEY

The Scrabble Game   Jan 1st 1983   #10

These projects assemble snapshots into collages to create fragmentary yet holistic images. The individual photos that make up the building blocks of each collage zoom in on individual details. By overlapping them, David Hockney is able to reconstruct the scene. For instance: at a glance, we see a family playing a game together at the table, but a closer look reveals that each player is caught in different moments and that the playing board is seen from more than one angle. The technique plays with our mind's instinctive tendency to create order and stories, inviting us to partake in the creation of the image while pointing out how fragmentary our experience of the world really is.

SCHRÖDINGER'S CAMERA

One location, different moments, physically layered and cut away with a scalpel

While at first glance they may appear to be digital, these visualizations are the results of an analog approach. Multiple photos were taken at the same location at different times. Michel Lamoller then made physical prints, stacked them in layers, and then cut pieces away using a scalpel. This method of combining multiple exposures enables the photographer to select which details from each moment should appear, actively shaping the resulting representation of time and space. In the end, it is the viewer who assembles multiple exposures into a single image based on the artist's edits.

MICHEL LAMOLLER

MANUFACTURED COINCIDENCES

Selective edits of multiple photos of the same
location to create imaginary scenarios

BABEL TALES_
PETER FUNCH

Photography can create a new reality just by editing ostensibly true images of the real world. Computer-assisted techniques open up a whole new range of possibilities, as seen in this series, in which Peter Funch took multiple unstaged photographs at the same location and then composited them, editing out all but one kind of detail from the surroundings. The images are both real and fictional at the same time. The method examines what it is that photography really depicts by working with repetition and juxtaposition. The project also explores how many commonalities we miss when we only see the world moment by moment.

ALL IN THE NOW

Minutes or even hours of activity collapsed into a few frames by separating the subject from the rest of the image

THE SAN DIEGO STUDIES
3 AND # 6 _
CY KUCKENBAKER

This series is interesting not just as an example of presenting multiple moments of an event in a single frame, but also as an example of a new form of visualization. These photos of a kite flying are actually stills from a video that collapses twenty minutes of action into a little more than one minute. Rather than just speeding up the action, Cy Kuckenbaker used post-processing to combine distinct moments from the kite's flight so that it executes all of its manoeuvres simultaneously. He used a similar technique to edit a video of midday traffic: all four color-coded images derive from the same original footage.

WHAT WAS THERE,
AND WHAT WAS NOT

Editing reality by compositing many photographs and removing all but the chosen details and individuals

While the photographs in this series are composites, Pelle Cass notes that "nothing has been changed, only selected." The photographer seeks to both order the world and exaggerate its chaos by taking multiple pictures at one location and then deciding which figures to leave in and which to remove. This editorial power can branch out in several directions: there is the possibility to create coincidences, like a park full of dogs or a tree full of squirrels, or to imagine a basketball game where single team seems to play against itself, or to go even further and use the real figures to create fictional stories and scenarios.

SELECTED PEOPLE_
PELLE CASS

HEAVIER THAN AIR

<u>Composite photography documenting
the day's events at one location</u>

WAKE TURBULENCE _
MIKE KELLEY

This photograph depicts "nearly a day's worth of aircraft movements merged into one visual experience." Though sourced from nearly 400 images of LAX, there are fewer than 400 events depicted here. By using compositing rather than a long exposure, the photographer can ensure that each event is rendered distinctly, while at the same time opening up the possibility of editing the source material to highlight certain relationships (one could choose to display only flights from a specific airline, for instance), to alter positioning or size to improve visibility, or to emphasize or deemphasize certain points.

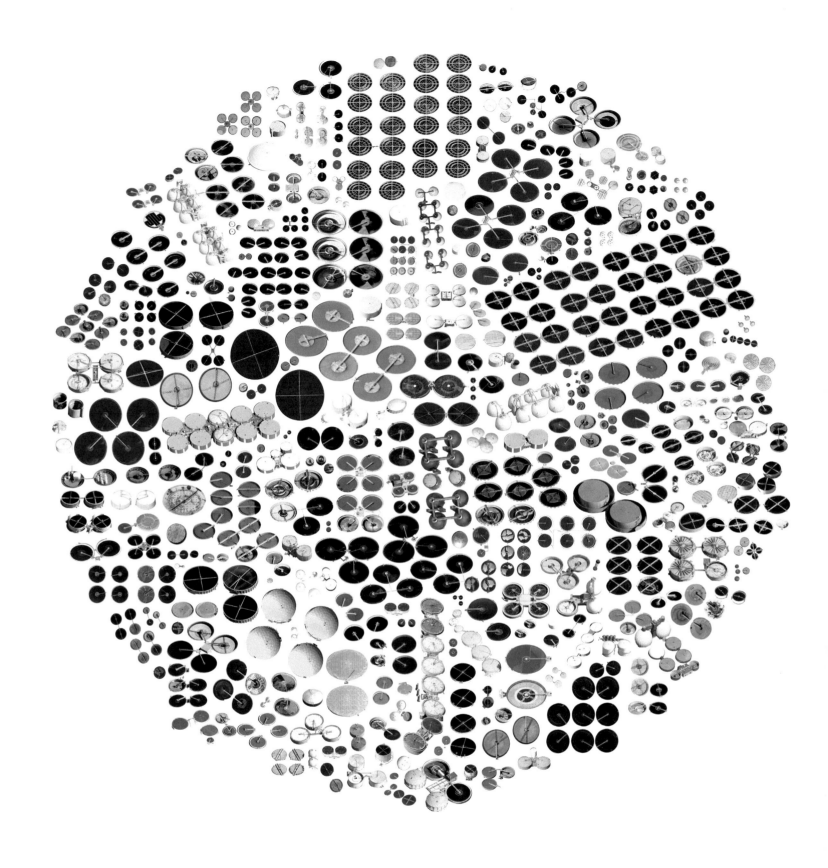

SHADOW BOXING THE WORLD

<u>Selected satellite imagery cut,</u>
<u>collected, and collaged</u>

Jenny Odell's visualizations are collages and collections built with publicly available satellite photographs from Google Maps. Using satellite images enables the artist to approach the visualizations from a normally impossible perspective and then to select what is depicted in the final image. Sets of specific objects or features are cut out and composited. Viewed together, the images question the effect of our human presence on Earth. They also represent a way in which the photographer can re-purpose existing photographs for entirely new uses. Where a satellite image shows a very general view, Odell's images are very specific.

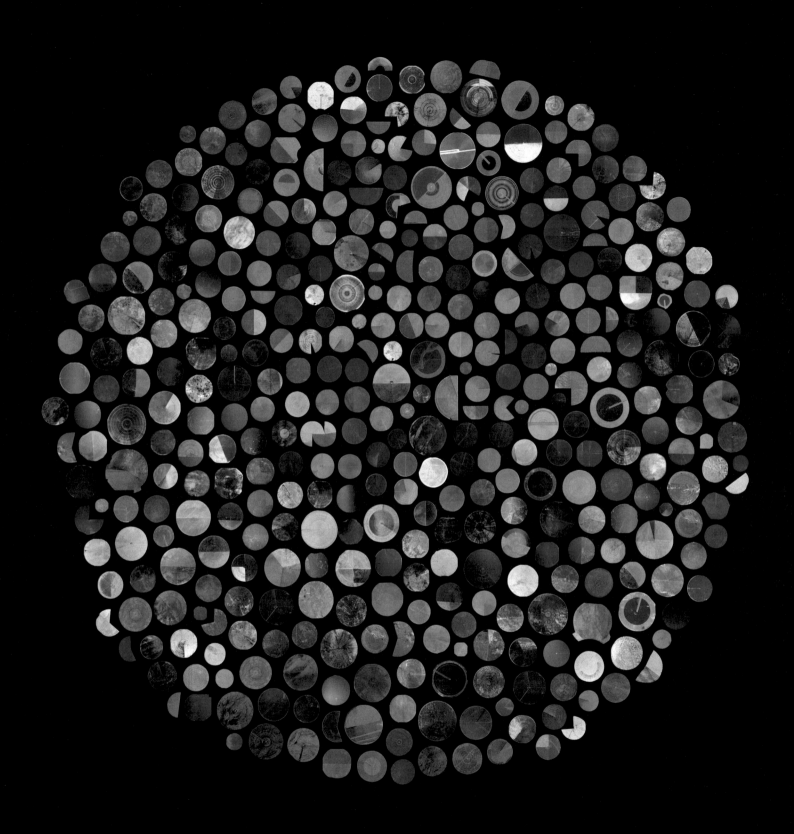

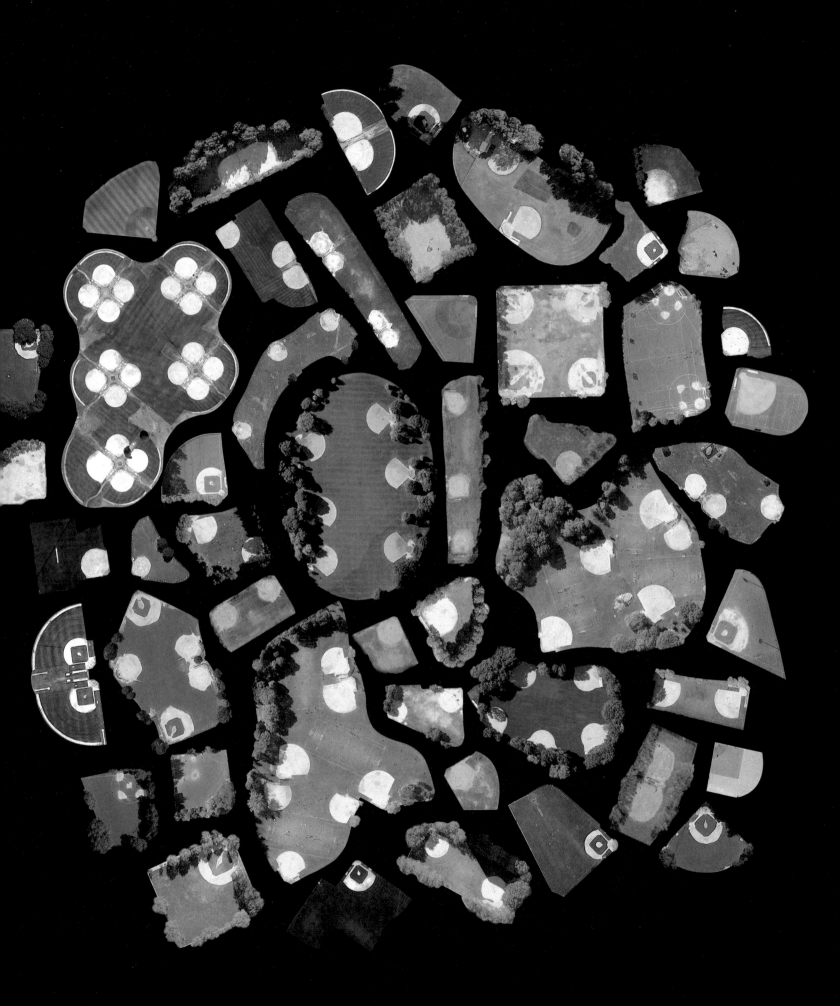

RIDING THE ESCHER EXPRESS

Videos of trains and carousels become warped, kaleidoscopic images with a bit of processing

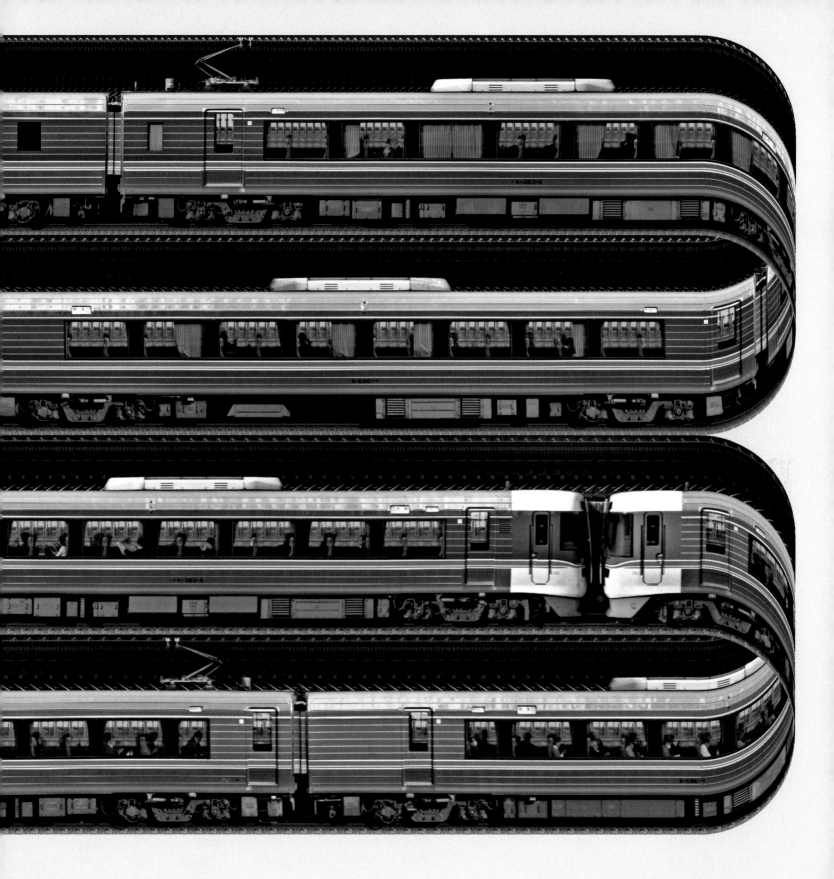

TRAINSCANS_
MASAKAZU MATSUMOTO

Using just an iPod touch and his TrainScanner program, Masakazu Matsumoto was able to create very long side-view photographs of passing trains that could then be twisted and contorted into new forms. The program stitches together a series of still images from a video—like slit-scan photography but without the special equipment. The resulting psychedelic images play with notions of space and time. Events and objects that would normally be too long to depict in a single photograph can be wrapped and re-packaged to fit in a single frame. The technique can be applied to other moving objects, like the spinning carousel that becomes a spiraling pinwheel.

DEGREES OF FROST

Composite satellite images of the snow cover
in the United States during one winter month

This massive photograph depicts the snow cover in the United States during February 2015. It is a composite of satellite images taken over a 28-day period and is part of a series that includes the two previous years. Tim Wallace has created images that can complement graphs or statistics about shifting weather conditions in a more immediate, visual way. The snow cover may be the result of separate events that may not have overlapped, but a composite image like this is able to show at a glance the cumulative effects. This technique also works as a form of cartography that repurposes satellite images.

A GIANT PICTURE OF
SNOW ACROSS THE
UNITED STATES _
TIM WALLACE

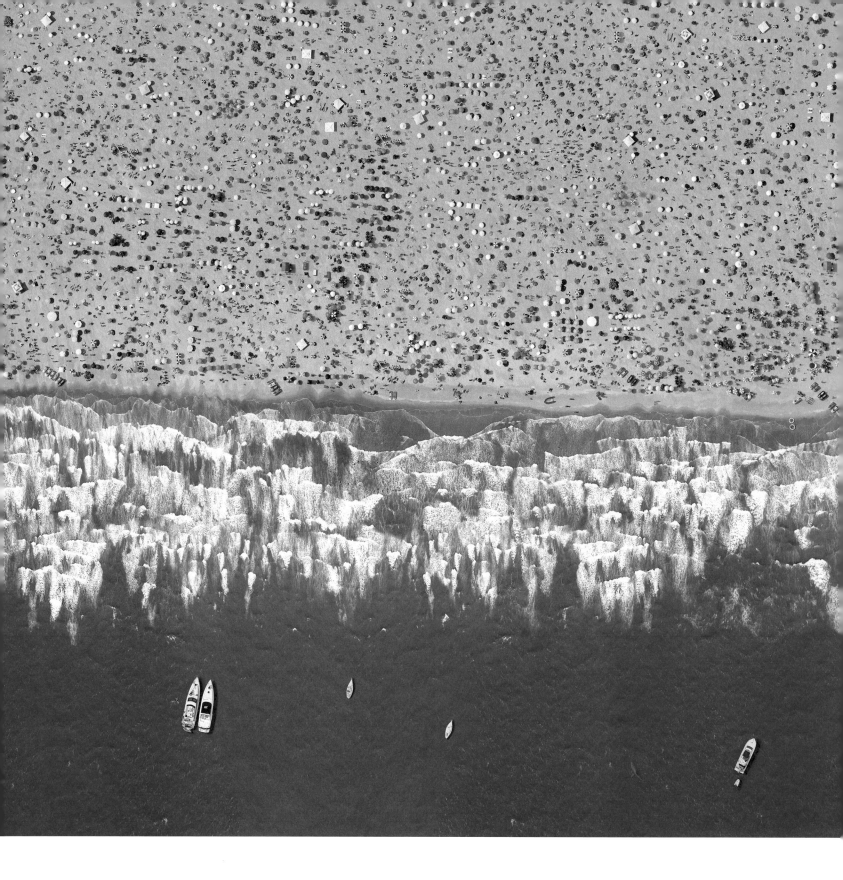

ROUGH FABRIC OF THE WORLD

Mosaics of constructed images form imaginary
aerial photographs rich in detail

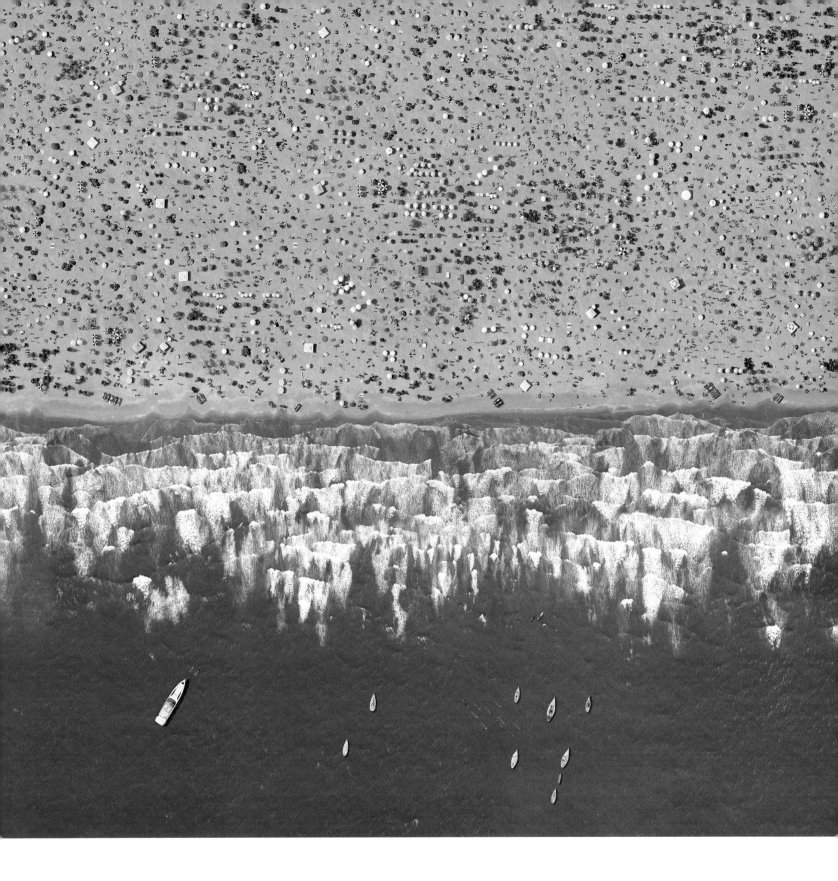

CÁSSIO VASCONCELLOS

In an effort to reveal the massive impact of human beings on the surface of the Earth, Cássio Vasconcellos used composite aerial photographs to create seamless panoramic mosaics that depict open spaces overwhelmed by people and manmade artefacts. Hundreds of different images come together to create imaginary landscapes—from afar they are rolls of texture, but up close, they are packed with detail. The photographs blend documentary realism with creative commentary: at their foundations they are composed of real images, but Vasconcellos combines and edits them—and exaggerates them—to emphasize the scale of human consumption.

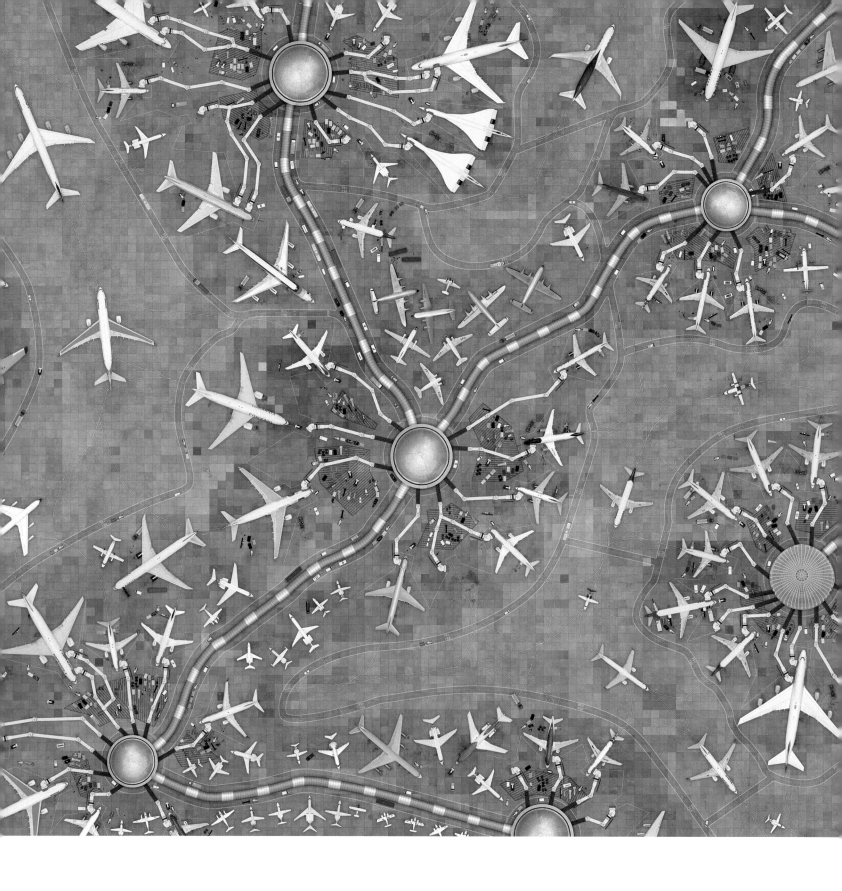

COLLECTIVES

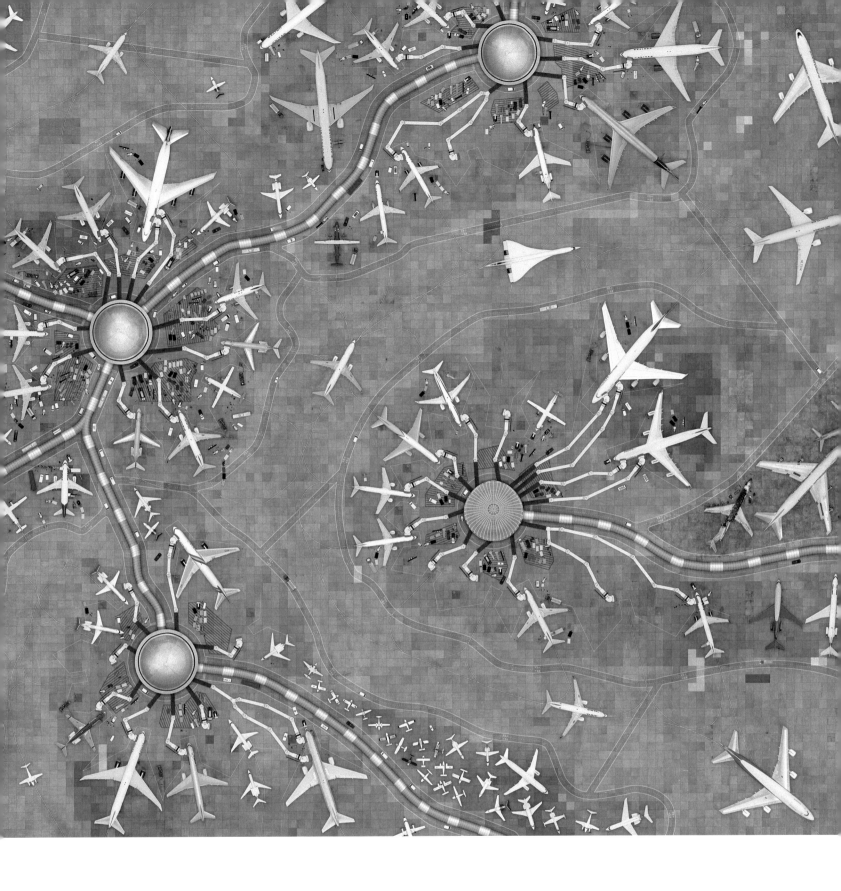

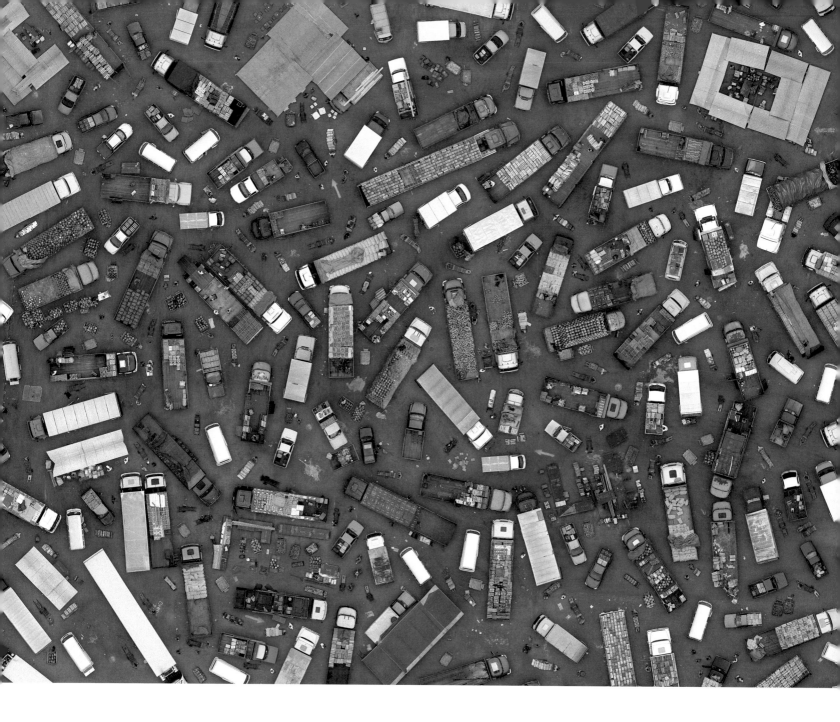

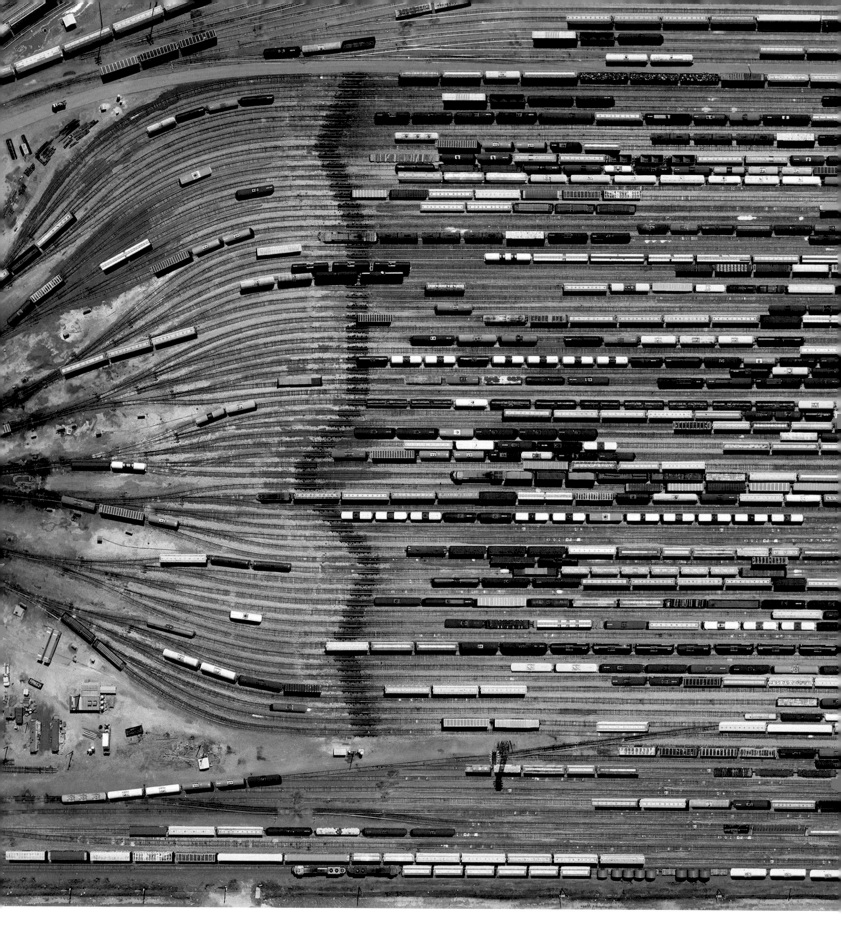

WELCOME TO THE ANTHROPOCENE

Composite and aerial photographs dramatize

the effects of growth and globalization

This series explores the global migration of people, goods, and services in the twenty-first century. Each carefully planned photograph depicts a real location but is composed of many images stitched together after the initial shooting. The resulting photographs are meant to provoke the viewer to question whether or how true the images are. The subversive manipulations of Marcus Lyon's images overcome our jadedness by playing with our expectations about photographs. As he says: "The world is too fabulously complicated for me to say what I want in a single shot. So I bring multiple images together to create a greater truth."

EXODUS_
MARCUS LYON

143

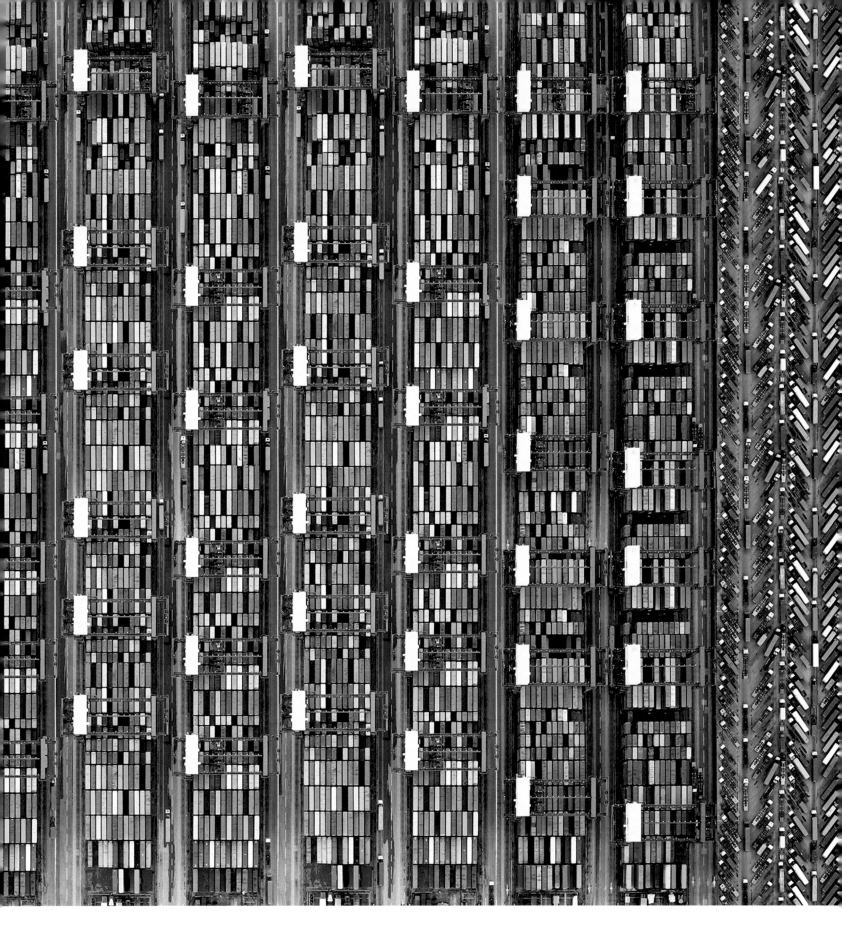

MARCUS LYON

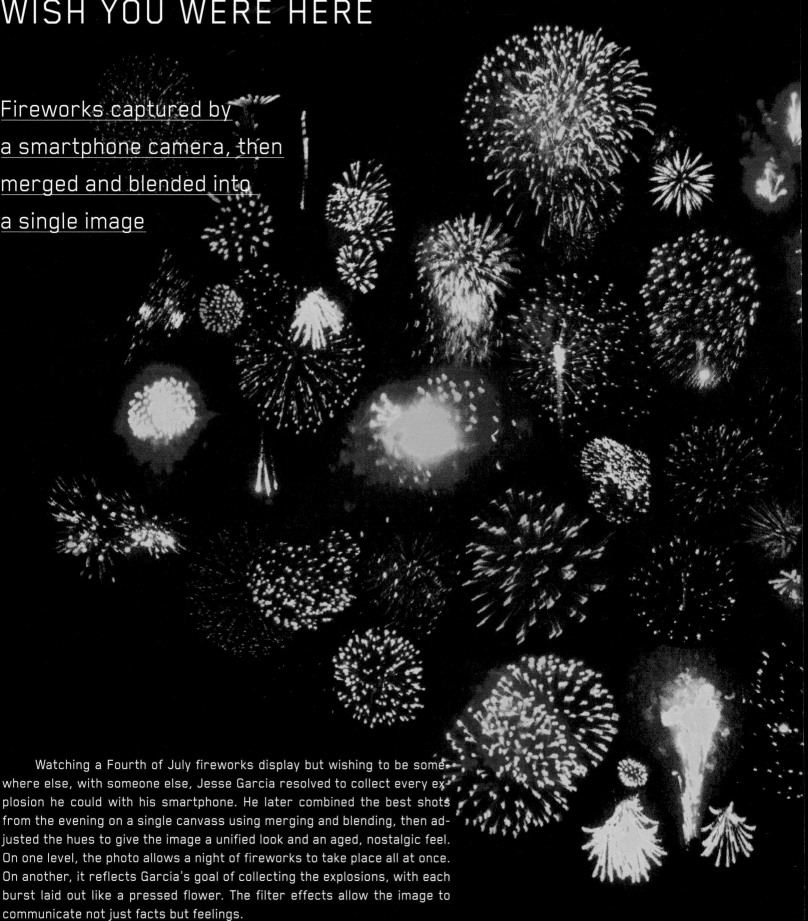

WISH YOU WERE HERE

Fireworks captured by
a smartphone camera, then
merged and blended into
a single image

Watching a Fourth of July fireworks display but wishing to be somewhere else, with someone else, Jesse Garcia resolved to collect every explosion he could with his smartphone. He later combined the best shots from the evening on a single canvass using merging and blending, then adjusted the hues to give the image a unified look and an aged, nostalgic feel. On one level, the photo allows a night of fireworks to take place all at once. On another, it reflects Garcia's goal of collecting the explosions, with each burst laid out like a pressed flower. The filter effects allow the image to communicate not just facts but feelings.

CONTACT SHEETS

Collections of all the things that people touched over 24 hours

Can a portrait be an example of PhotoViz? And must a portrait always feature a headshot of the subject? The photographs in Paula Zuccotti's series are informative, evocative portraits of individuals ranging from preschoolers to traditional musicians. They depict the personalities and daily routines of their subjects without ever actually showing the subjects themselves. Instead, Zucotti creates a photographic collage of all the objects that each one touched over the course of a day. The results are rich in information and narratives, and, because the subjects are absent, the viewer is actively challenged to interpret them.

EVERY THING WE TOUCH _
PAULA ZUCCOTTI

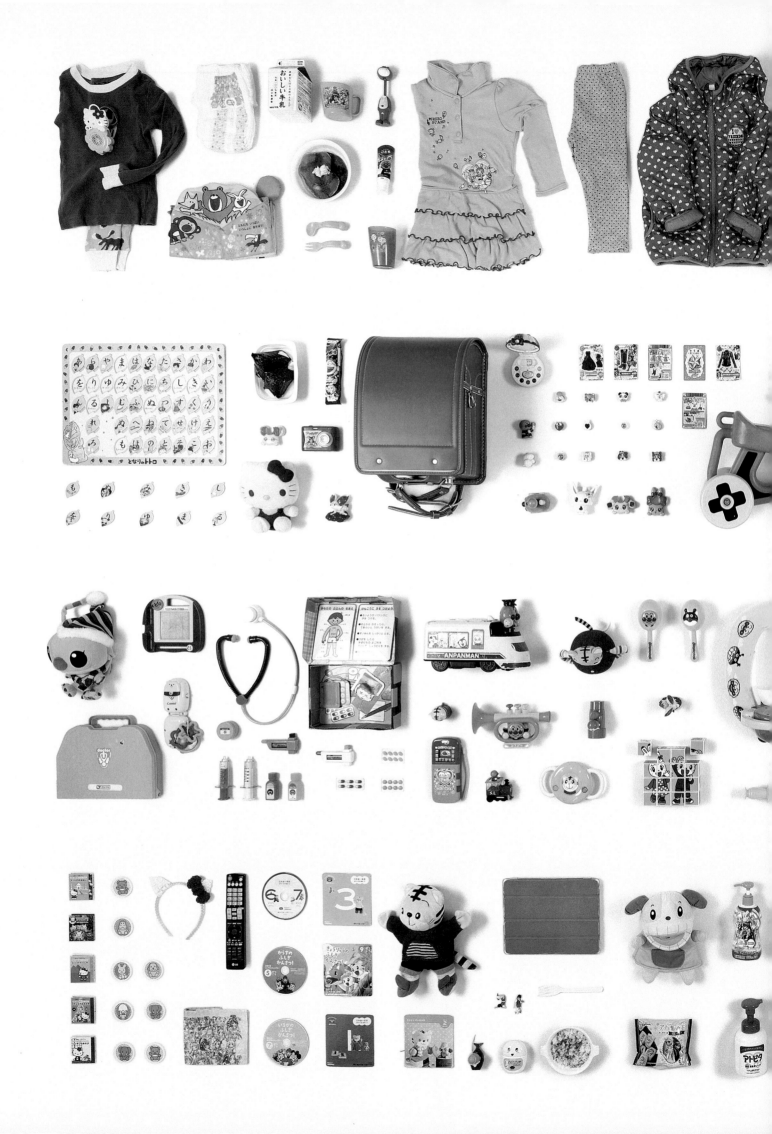

RECYCLING PROGRAM

Photos of on-site installations reveal the impact of plastic waste on a nature reserve

Composition is an important aspect of any photograph—and of any visualization. While some photographers carefully arrange the content of their images during post-processing, in this case, Alejandro Durán chose to set the scene first. The project addresses the problem of pollution washing ashore at Sian Ka'an, Mexico, a federal nature reserve and UNESCO World Heritage Site. Durán created an installation by sorting the waste by color and then used the visual language of nature and landscape photography to dramatize the incursion of pollution into the natural world. The photos are carefully composed storytelling devices.

WASHED UP:
TRANSFORMING A
TRASHED LANDSCAPE _
ALEJANDRO DURÁN

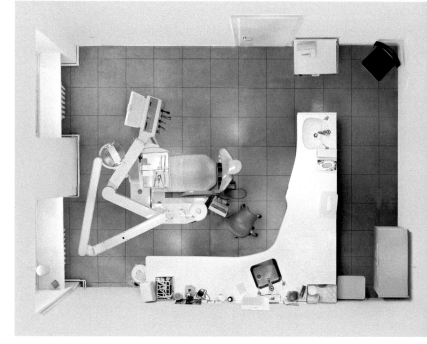

A MODEL EXISTENCE

Multiple top-down photos stitched together yield novel perspectives on our living spaces

Beyond time and motion, perspective can be a powerful tool for visualization. By enabling us to view things from impossible or unusual positions, photography can reveal new insights and impressions. In this case, Menno Aden flattens the interiors of real living and working spaces into 2D scale models by stitching together 10 to 1,000 images taken top-down from above by remote control. The technique is akin to removing the ceiling and replacing it with a scanner. The results reveal hidden symmetrical compositions and the way the (absent) inhabitants exist in their enclosed spaces.

HOUSES OF THE HOLY

<u>Vertical panoramas capture
the full span of the interiors of
churches arcing from front to back</u>

VERTICAL CHURCHES_
RICHARD SILVER

Seeking a way to capture the full scope of a church's interior architecture, Richard Silver hit upon the idea of turning the panoramic technique on its side. From the middle of the aisle, the camera pans from the altar, across the ceiling, and back down to the entrance. Scanning the photos from bottom to top replicates the feel of craning one's head up and back, trying to take it all in. Not only do the visualizations yield a wealth of architectural information, by including so many related elements in one frame rather than breaking them up into separate photos—they also convey the impression of being present at each site.

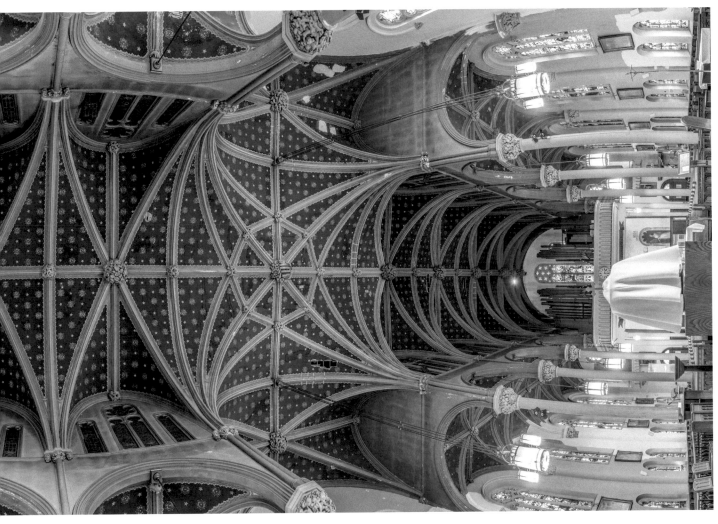

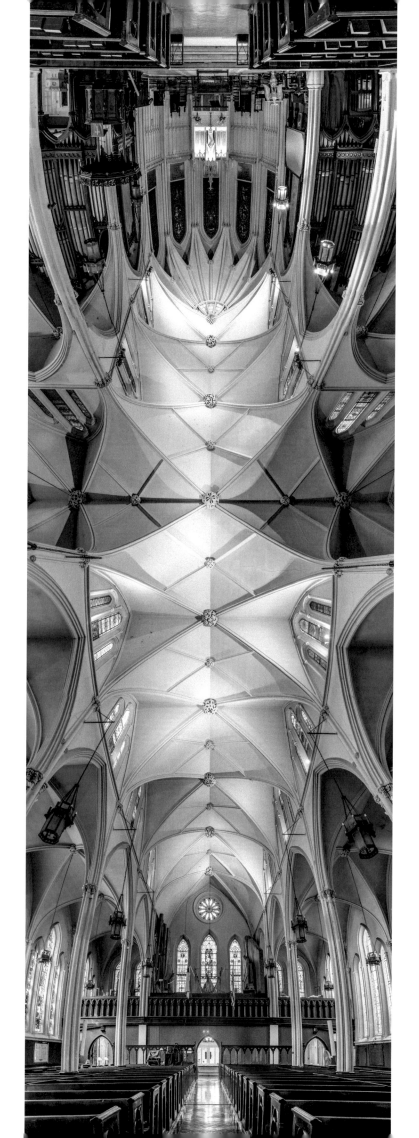

STANDING THE
WORLD ON ITS HEAD

Composite photography
creates rooms that seem to be
photographed from below

By photographing the undersides of individual objects and then creating digital composite images, Michael H. Rohde creates the illusion of rooms viewed from below while looking up through a glass floor. The images are disorienting at first. Presenting what should be impossible views, they turn the objects and spaces that make up everyday life on their heads, inviting us to reconsider our relationships with them. This technique shows how radical image compositing can be: The objects in each image have been photographed individually and recombined to create a room. Not only the perspectives but also the spaces themselves have been constructed with photographic techniques.

FROM BELOW_
MICHAEL H. ROHDE

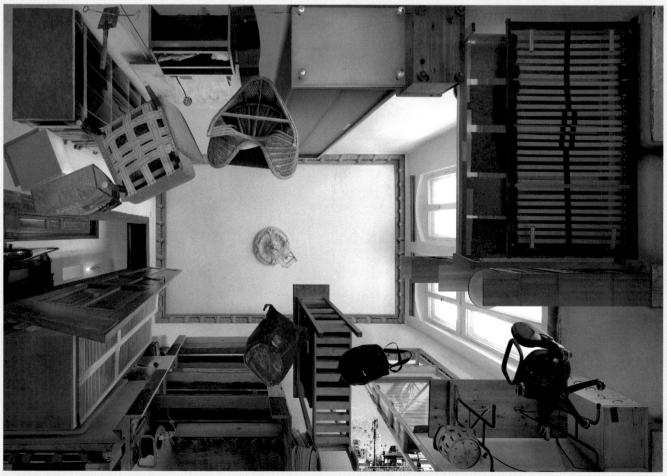

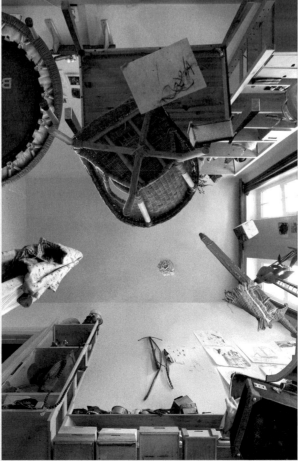

MICHAEL H. ROHDE

FAULT LINES AND FRACTURES

Automobile accidents leave traces that
nocturnal long-exposure photographs reveal

SCARS _
LUCAS ZIMMERMANN

Human tragedies leave indelible marks on our surroundings, which we often fail to see or consider. Lucas Zimmermann set out to document some of these scars by taking long-exposure photographs of sections of guardrails that were replaced following accidents. The new sections are lighter, and by taking photographs head-on with lights shining directly at the guardrails—a perspective that we rarely have as we drive—he succeeds in bringing out the stark contrast between the tissue of the road and the wound that has healed but not entirely disappeared. A shift in perspective and focus can be a powerful storytelling tool.

LUCAS ZIMMERMANN

SHADOWS OF LOSS

Pre-Second World War photos projected
onto buildings in a former Jewish quarter

These images are photographs of an art installation staged on the streets of Berlin's former Jewish quarter. Shimon Attie slide-projected portions of photographs of Jewish street life in Berlin in the years before the Second World War onto the facades of buildings where they had been taken. Visible to the current residents and passersby, the fragmentary projections brought pieces of the past back to life. There are two photo visualizations at work here: the immersive projection of the past onto the present, which visitors experienced, and these documentary photographs, which bring those recreations to a larger audience.

THE WRITING ON
THE WALL_
SHIMON ATTIE

Beggars Parade — Freetown

PICTURE FRAMES

Old postcards placed over new photos of the same locations

O N C E   S A L O N E :
F R E E T O W N ' S   T H E N
A N D   N O W _
B A B A K   F A K H A M Z A D E H

By juxtaposing old postcards from colonial-era Freetown, Sierra Leone, with photographs of the same locations taken in the present day, Babak Fakhamzadeh opens a portal to the past. The white borders of the postcards become window frames, and we are able to peer back in time. The comparisons reveal not only urban development and construction but also shifts in social and economic conditions. Matching past and present required research and a bit of luck, as changes over the decades rendered parts of the city unrecognizable. Access to online maps and archives makes this technique available to photographers around the world.

Mill Street, Freetown

Lisk-Carew Bro
Photo, Freetown

NICHOLS BRIDGE, FREETOWN, SIERRA LEONE

THERE IN ARCADIA

Computer graphics overlays
simulate views of nature
meditated or enhanced by modern
technology

    This series explores the possibilities inherent in the picture-in-picture technique utilized by Babak Fakhamzadeh on the preceding pages. Marc Dorf's hybrids of photography and computer graphics point to ways that photographs may be enriched in the future, ranging from variations on the idea of overlapping photos, or images inserted into other images, to the integration of more abstract graphical elements that reference or even employ data visualization. As the digital manipulation of photographs takes on increasing importance, these images strive for a new visual language that combines the natural and the virtual.

// _ P A T H _
M A R C   D O R F

C C T V
D O C U M E N T A R Y   I D E N T S _
J L   D E S I G N   A N D   K O R B

OUT OF THIS CLAY

Motion sculptures built with post-processing and motion capture

These combinations of motion capture and post-processing render motion and time into concrete, sculptural shapes. The flow of movement is retained, though abstracted, making it possible to trace the course of the dancers though space and along an axis of time. That progression is rendered in a kind of physical, sculptural form resembling wood or stone. The actors were captured using Sony PlayStation cameras and iPiSoft, which allowed them to move unencumbered while still yielding the degree of data necessary for the intensive post-production work. This technique finds a way to give physical form to something ephemeral.

NATURE OF THE BEAST

Slit-scan photography as a tool
for reimagining the human form

M E T A M O R P H O S E _
F R É D É R I C   F O N T E N O Y

Slit-scan photography works by capturing just a sliver of the subject at a time and then assembling those highly detailed slices afterwards. Frédéric Fontenoy uses it here to deliberately distort the human form. Because the body is moving as the scan occurs, it is weirdly, glitchily stretched losing a head while gaining an arm, or fragmenting into disembodied limbs. Slit-scan photography is meant to be a means of achieving highly precise images. This process represents a way in which photographic techniques can be removed from their intended areas of application and used in unintended ways to achieve novel visual effects.

UNDER CONSTRUCTION

Extremely long camera exposures document urban development

Some long exposures last only a second, others last a few minutes or even hours. In this case, the exposure lasted for years. Michael Wesely began his project in the mid-1990s, attempting to document urban development in photos showing one location and perspective over time. By using filters and small apertures to decrease the amount of light reaching the film, he could leave the shutter open for very long time periods—in theory, for decades. New buildings and construction equipment appear as ghostly images. We often think of the past as hazy and the present as distinct, but here that perspective is reversed.

NEW URBAN FABRIC _
MICHAEL WESELY

THE VIEW FROM HYPERSPACE

Slit-scan photography turns moving objects into static tableaus and blurs stationary details into speeding lines

Using non-traditional photographic gear of his own design and processing the visual data with programs that he developed himself, Adam Magyar stretches and freezes time. What seems like a distorted panorama of a crowd is really a sum of the people who passed in front of the lens of his slit-scan camera. At the far right are those who passed first; those at the far left are those who passed last—and all of them actually occupy the same point of space. The highly detailed photo of the subway is also not a panorama: it is a slice-by-slice scan of the train as it sped past the lens of Magyar's line scan device.

URBAN FLOW
AND STAINLESS_
ADAM MAGYAR

200

BLURRING THE LINES

Long-exposure photos from
the window of a speeding train

The confluence of speed, curves, and time results in abstracted images that smooth the surroundings and paint them
all with blurred brushstrokes sweeping in the same direction.
Céline Ramoni Lee positioned the camera close to the window
to remove reflections and used exposure times of 0.2 to 0.8
seconds. This technique places the viewer directly in the middle
of the action: it visualizes not the motion of the subject but the
motion of the observer. Rather than depicting a speeding train,
the photos visualize the experience of speed and motion. The
physical details blur away, allowing the images to document a
sensation instead.

LONG EXPOSURE_
CÉLINE RAMONI LEE

STOP AND GO

The rhythms of urban life
emerge in long-exposure photos

Cities around the world are alive with rushing traffic and bustling crowds, but they are not in perpetual motion. The individuals and vehicles that make up the cells of each city adopt a rhythm that is in sync with their surroundings, one unique to each metropolis. Martin Roemers's long-exposure photographs capture these moments of stasis and flow, as trains become indistinct walls and pedestrians swirl like fog around stationary vendors and shoppers on the lookout for bargains. This series demonstrates that it is not just what is in motion that matters in long-exposure visualization, but also what remains still.

BROAD BRUSHSTROKES

Paint spilled at an intersection tracks traffic patterns

While many examples of PhotoViz are documentary in nature, it is sometimes necessary for the photographer to intervene in the scene to achieve the desired result. In this case, IEPE set out to map the life and motion of an intersection in Berlin. By spilling paint on the road, he was able to visually document the paths of the drivers, cyclists, and pedestrians who passed through it. On one level, the project is a kind of group-painting on an urban canvas. On another, it is like a live-action long-exposure photograph in which the paint on the asphalt takes the place of chemical reactions in the emulsion.

PAINTING REALITY_
IEPE

GOING PLACES

Traffic in a blacked-out
London lit only by headlights

An urban blackout represents an exciting opportunity for photographers interested in documenting the flow of life and traffic in a city. With its electrical supply cut off, virtually the only illumination in London came from automobile headlights and individuals with flashlights. In long-exposure photographs, the streets seem to be drawn with rapid, confident white pen strokes, while the less certain, wavering lines of flashlights hint at the locations of sidewalks. Features of the surroundings also emerge from the darkness, like the silhouetted streetlights. The result is a kind of negative or reversed image of the city.

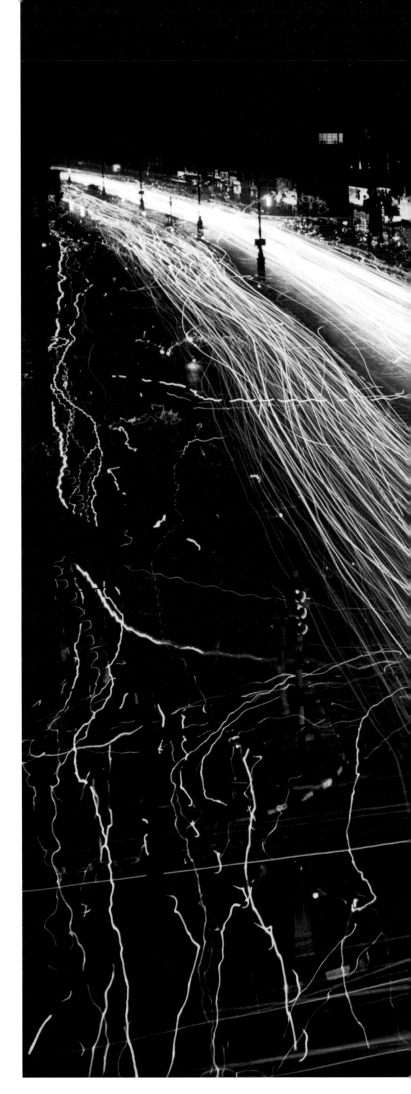

LONDON BLACKOUT_
WALTER BELLAMY

INSERT COIN

Long-exposure photographs
of arcade games from the 1980s

Rosemarie Fiore captured complex patterns in old-school arcade games by taking long-exposure photographs as she played through them. By documenting a whole game or session in a single frame of film, she revealed structures and patterns that are intrinsic to the games and yet not normally visible to us. Each vector-based game produced its own distinct series of images, with lines and kaleidoscopic shapes oriented around a center point. The photographs resemble kinematic fingerprints identifying each game. They flatten an entire experience of play into a 2D design, a kind of map of the photographer's time in cyberspace.

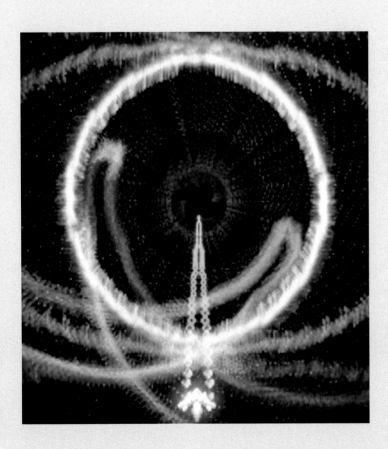

RETROGAME TIME LAPSE_
ROSEMARIE FIORE

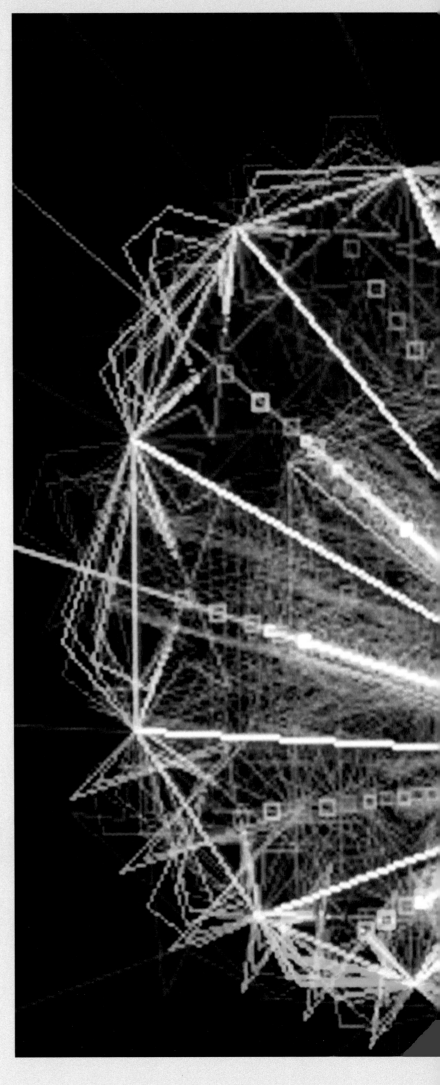

GOOD VIBRATIONS

LED lights with custom
color patterns and long-exposure
photography tell tales of
movement

M O T I O N   E X P O S U R E _
S T E P H E N   O R L A N D O

Intentionally equipping the subject with lights allows the photographer to choose what aspect of the subject's motion will be tracked and visualized, and to control how it is done. Using colored lights can be an aesthetic choice or a way to better distinguish or emphasize specific features of the subject. In the first examples, the actual subject has disappeared due to the long exposure, leaving one to wonder what is visualized while placing the emphasis on the (abstract) results. In the latter example, the density of information is greater because it is clear at a glance what is being visualized.

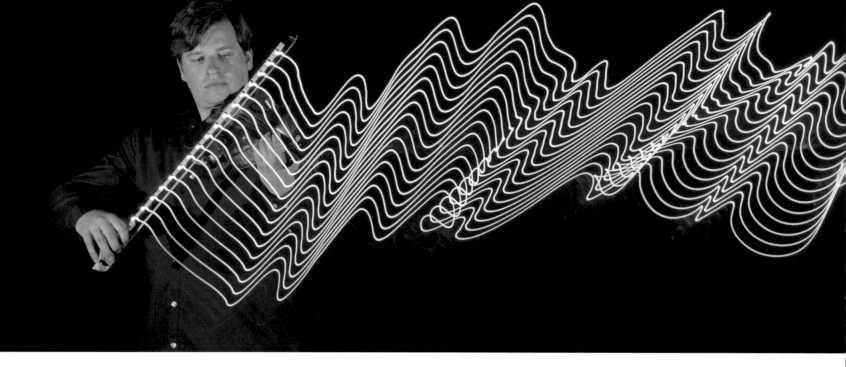

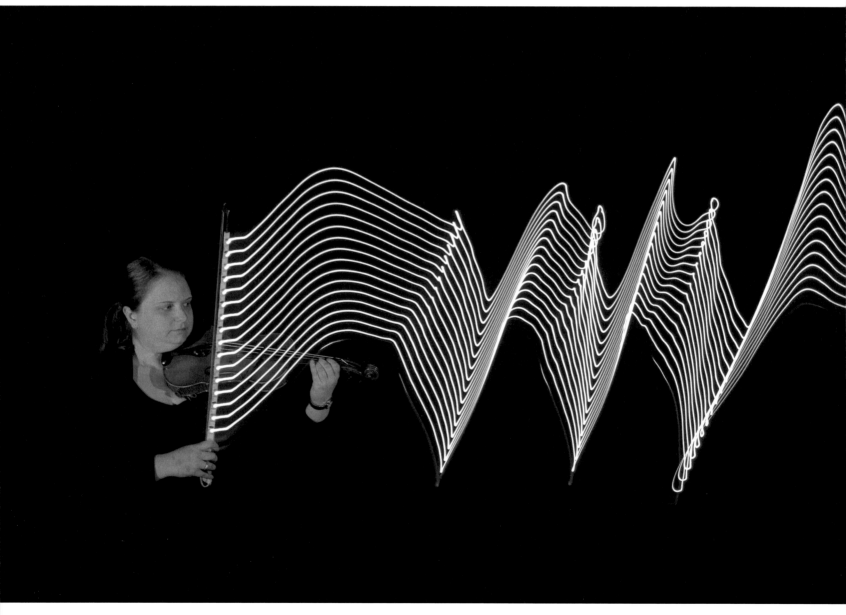

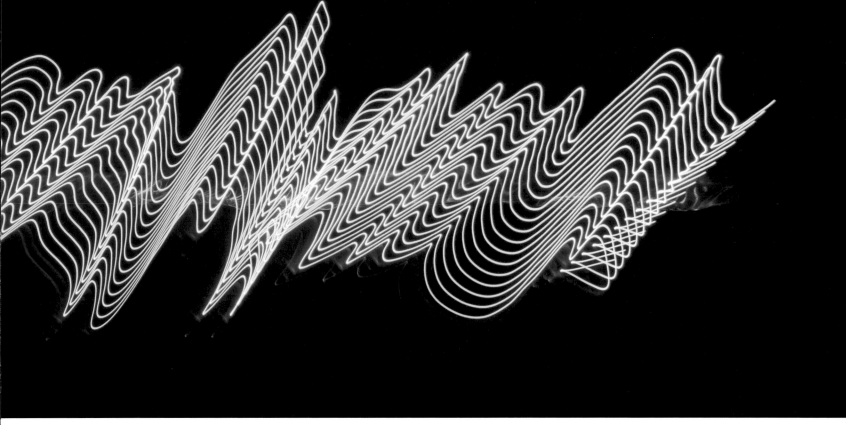

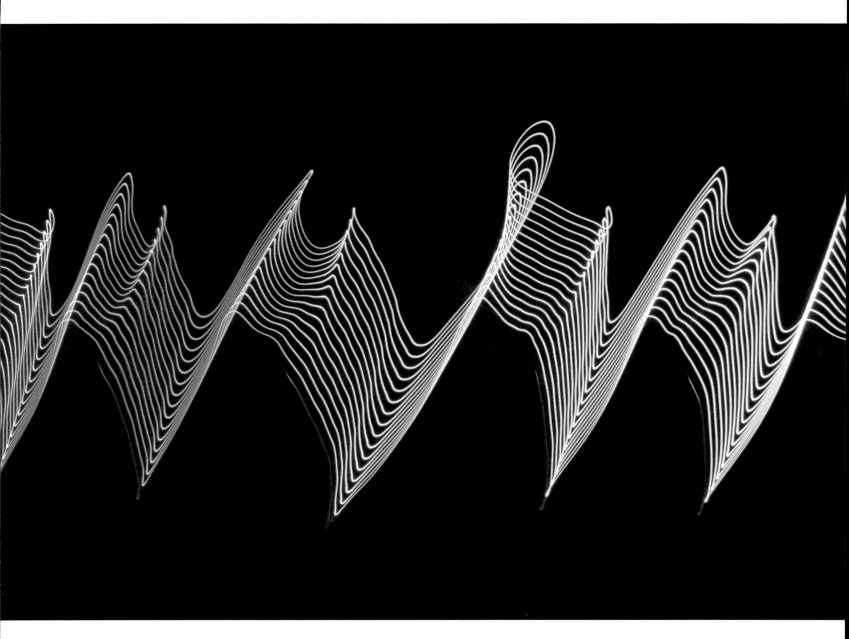

MARS ATTACKS

Long-exposure photographs
of carnival rides in action

CARNIVAL _
ROGER VAIL

Working with long exposures is a way of seeing the world from new perspectives, a way of stepping outside our normal experience of time. But for that reason, the technique may also yield surprising or unexpected results that only become apparent after the image is processed. Despite careful preparation, the results may still be matters of chance. Roger Vail uses a vintage camera to photograph carnival rides. The results—swirls of color, ethereal architecture, glowing UFOs—rival imaginative computer graphics, yet are produced without special effects. The process is as much a journey of discovery as it is an experiment in visualization.

ROGER VAIL

SPRAY PAINTING

Fog and long exposures turn
traffic lights into jets of color

T R A F F I C   L I G H T S _
L U C A S   Z I M M E R M A N N

A lonely road, traffic lights, fog, a camera: Lucas Zimmermann says that these images explore the way that a familiar object can create "a strong graphic effect in an unnatural situation with a simple photographic setup." The colors of the lights in the fog caught his eye by chance and the long exposure photographs that he stopped to make emphasize the sort of details and effects that we often overlook. A snapshot would also have captured the colors, but the choice of long exposure brings the glow to the forefront, capturing the mood as well. As a result, the images look the way the scene felt.

FLY BY WIRE

Long exposures reveal and document invisible paths and corridors

This series reveals the flight paths of the more than one million aircraft that pass through the skies over London each year. By shooting with exposures up to one hour long, Joel James Devlin was able to track multiple aircraft in a single frame, revealing their shared flight paths while also abstracting the images into something new. The cabin lights create smooth vector lines, while the flashing wing lights rhythmically indicate relative distance and speed. If the subject of a visualization has a light source attached to it, it is possible to create these kinds of abstracted views depicting precise paths though time and space.

AVIATION VECTORS_
JOEL JAMES DEVLIN

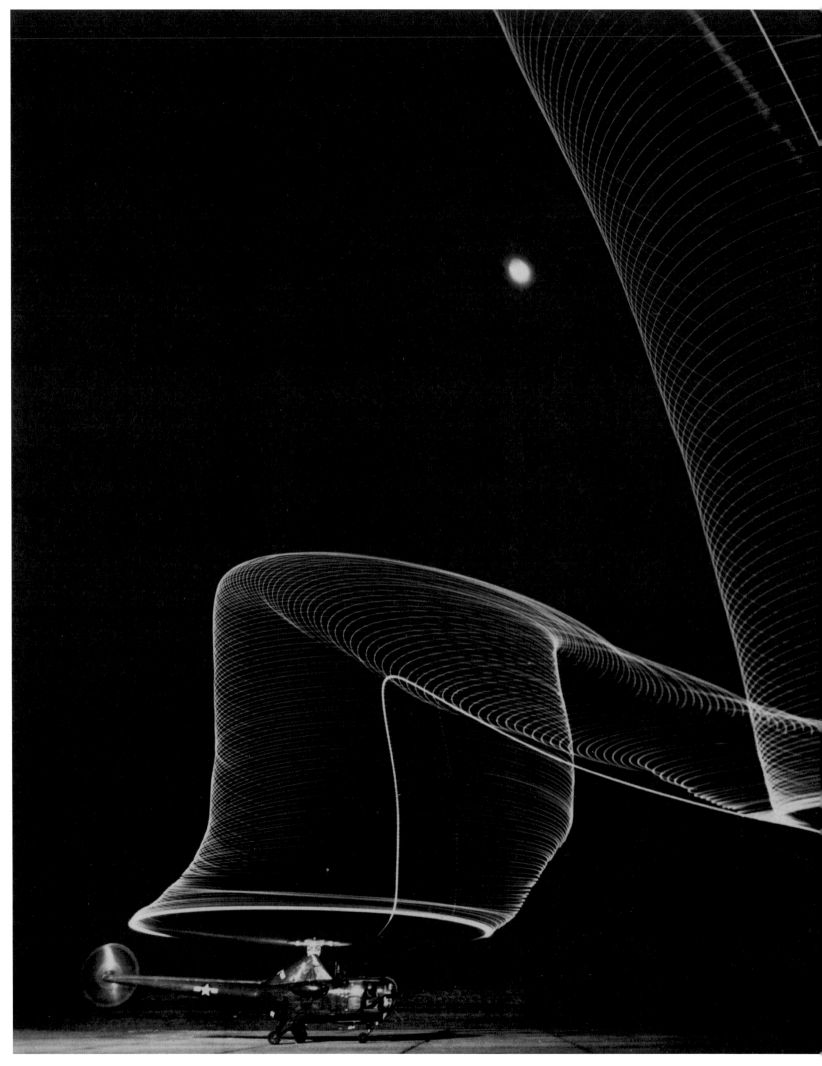

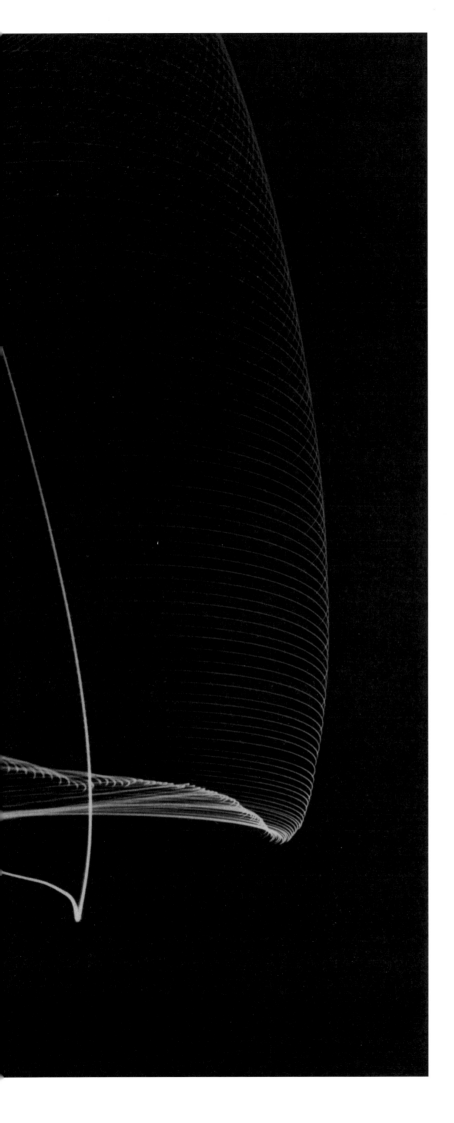

AND SOULS SET FREE

The spirals and curves of a helicopter's ascent were captured by a long exposure in 1949

Analog photo visualization techniques can produce timeless images. This series was produced in 1949 but still feels fresh today. Two simultaneous and related motions are tracked using long exposures and lights: that of a light on a helicopter's rotor and of a light on the helicopter itself. The revolving rotor becomes a kind of bouncing spring, while the point of light representing the helicopter is transported up and through the resulting tunnel. Andreas Feininger's image also includes a stationary image of the subject, a useful technique that allows the viewer to immediately recognize what is being visualized.

NIGHTTIME LONG EXPOSURES OF ROTATING HELICOPTER BLADES _
ANDREAS FEININGER

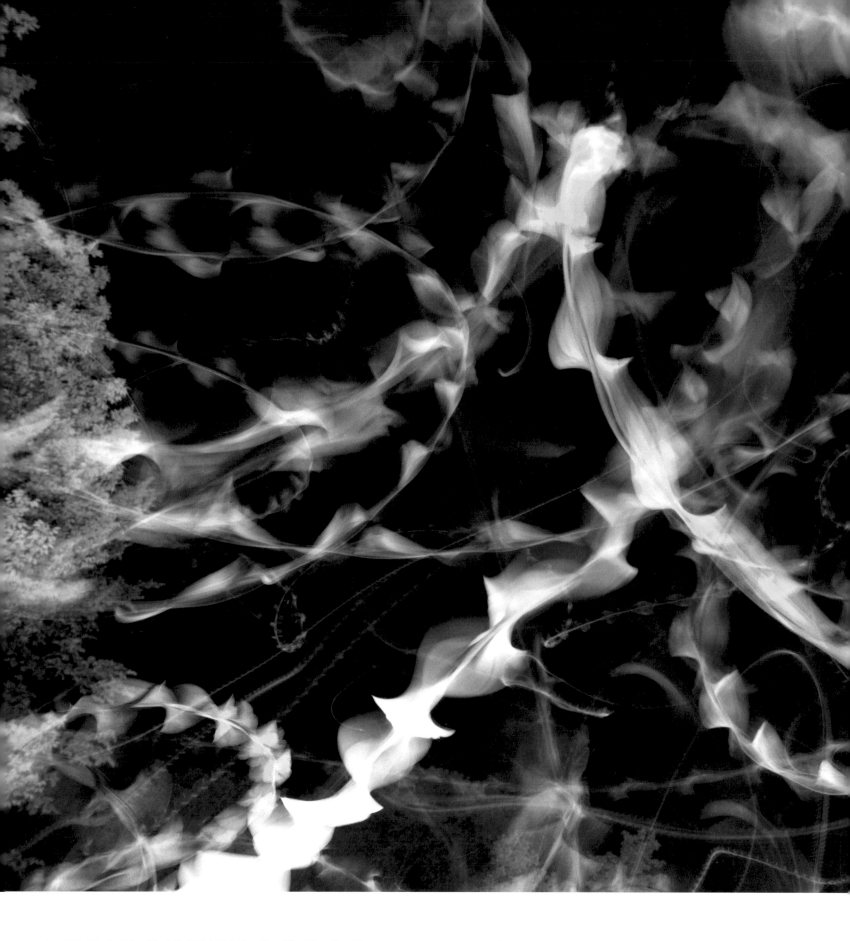

LEPIDOPTEROGRAPHY

Long-exposure photographs tracking
the flight paths of moths attracted to light

MOTHS TO LIGHT/
FIREFLIES AND STAR
TRAILS_
STEVE IRVINE

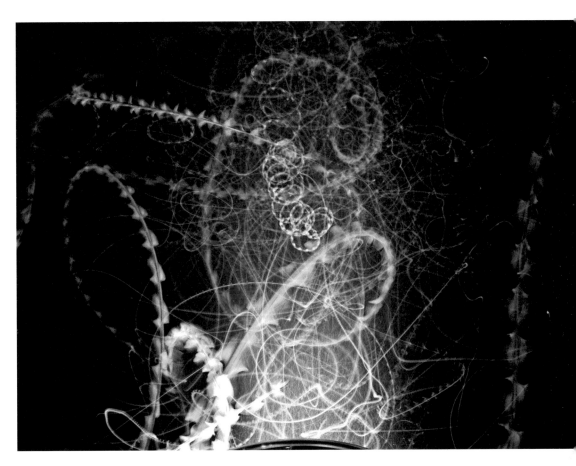

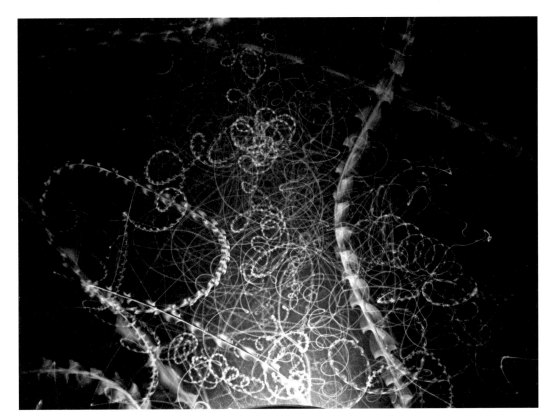

Using long-exposure photography it is possible to document the unseen while creating abstract, artistic images. Steve Irvine's photos reveal not only the surprisingly complex flight paths of moths, but also describe the patterns made by their flapping wings. At the same time, the blurring resulting from the long exposures abstracts the moths into swirling brush strokes or tendrils of smoke, which invite the viewer to rediscover the physical world from a higher perspective or longer time frame. The final image depicts one hour of firefly flashes and star trails. At the right time scale, the insects become stars as well.

FIRE AND BRIMSTONE

A nighttime battle lit by tracers and
captured by long exposures

Taken at night, this long-exposure photograph shows U.S. troops stationed at a base in Vietnam combatting a sniper in the surrounding hills during the Vietnam War. The red lines are tracer bullets fired from M60 machine guns. The white lines are tracers fired by a tank equipped with two 40-mm auto cannon; the small white bursts are from a .50-caliber machine gun. Tracers enable observers to see where a gun is firing at night, but make up only a fraction of the total rounds fired. The amount of ordnance in the air is five times greater than the photo can depict. An image full of force and fire, it reminds us that war is hell.

NIGHT FIRE_
JAMES SPEED
HENSINGER

THEY WERE NEVER REALLY THERE

Using moving LEDs and long exposures to build sculptures out of light

    The motion of artificial light can be used to erect structures that are real in the sense that they interact with their surroundings even though they only exist in the resulting photographs. Long exposures enable the photographer to draw lines with light, which move, shine, and cast shadows in a natural three-dimensional environment. Even though they are artificial, the light sculptures have a realness and physicality that computer generated images would lack. The technique can be used to visualize structures or landscape features that are absent or planned, as well as to enhance or emphasize the environment with sculptures or monuments.

TRANSIENT LIGHT _
MARTIN KIMBELL

MARTIN KIMBELL

PHOTO GRAPHÊ

Picasso drawing with a light
and long-exposure photographs

P A B L O   P I C A S S O _
G J O N   M I L I

Photographic pioneer Gjon Mili attached lights to the skates of figure skaters and left the shutter on his camera open. In those long-exposure photographs, the skaters seemed to draw abstract curves and lines through space. After sharing the photos with Picasso, the painter grabbed a flashlight and began tracing drawings of his own in the air. Mili's photographs capture the artist at work, mid-stroke, as his creations glow and hover before him. This technique turns the surroundings into a canvas that can be drawn on or around. At the same time, it straddles the line between being a work of art and documenting the act of creation.

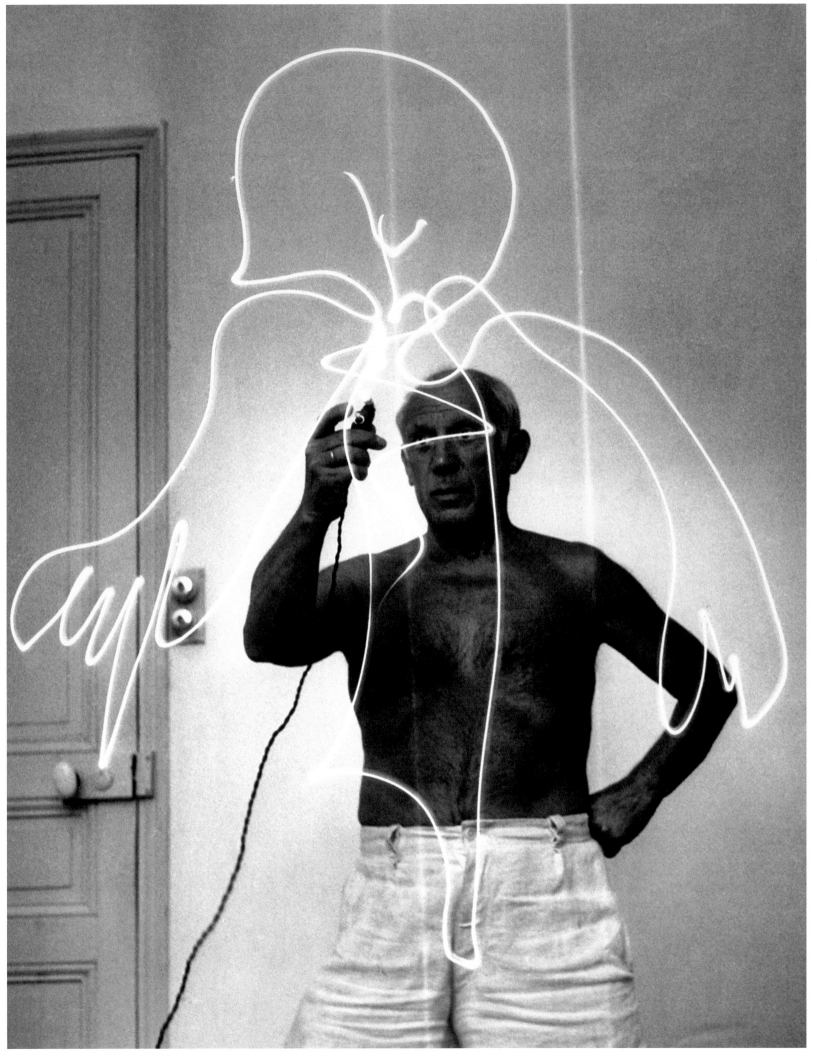

SET IT ALL ABLAZE

A combination of fireworks,
long exposures, and post-processing

Light snakes and curls across the surface of twisted trees as sparks fall from the branches like pouring water. These impermanent sculptures exist only as photographs. ND filters balance the oncoming darkness and the flaring light of the fireworks, which were manually waved around the trees. Long exposures turned the flares into fluid lines and the sparks into streamers, while post-processing enabled Vitor Schietti to combine several takes into a single image. Careful planning and experimentation were required, as there was less than an hour each evening when the light conditions were ideal for this type of photography.

IMPERMANENT SCULPTURES
VITOR SCHIETTI

TERRA INCOGNITA

Long exposures, LED lights, and a signal detector used to visualize the invisible terrain of Wi-Fi networks

I M M A T E R I A L S :
L I G H T   P A I N T I N G   W I F I _
T I M O   A R N A L L   E T   A L .

As Walter Mitchel wrote, we have constructed an "electro-magnetic terrain" of networking and communications hotspots, dead spots, and varying signal strengths. The terrain is invisible and is only hinted at by antennas or wireless routers, yet we move through it each day. Arnall, Knutsen, and Martinussen devised a way to make that terrain visible using long-exposure photography and LED lights attached to a device capable of measuring Wi-Fi signal strength. The greater the signal, the higher the lights rise on the vertical axis. By moving the device they were able to reveal the presence and variety of those signals in public urban spaces.

LIGHT RAIL TRANSIT

<u>Long-exposure photographs of a tram</u>
<u>covered in thousands of LEDs</u>

CHRISTMAS TRAM_
ZSOLT ANDRASI

Budapest's public transportation agency decorated an old tram for Christmas, covering it with more than forty thousand LEDs. Zsolt Andrasi set out to capture the tram as it arrived at and departed from a stop. With exposure times of up to 42 seconds, the tram itself disappears and only the glowing trails of the LEDs remain visible, tracing the path it follows through the city at night. The decorations were meant to liven up the holiday season by creating a "tram of light." The photographs make that notion real—the long exposures and the LEDs abstract the form of the tram, leaving only the impression it created.

AND BOMBS BURSTING IN AIR

Adjusting focus during long exposures makes fireworks bloom

There is a simple trick behind these dreamlike images of fireworks that seem to pulse and swell like strange undersea creatures or exotic, spiky fruits. It is all a matter of focus. David Johnson took long exposures lasting a second or two—but each shot was intentionally out of focus at first. When he heard the explosion, he would quickly refocus. As a result, the early stages of the explosion are diffuse balls and blurry triangles, while the later stages appear as sharp points and lines. It is a simple technique, entirely in-camera, and yet it produces results that look very different from typical images of streaking fireworks.

FIREWORKS_
DAVID JOHNSON

INDEX

/

Courtesy of MIT
Museum.
P : 4

ELIASSON, OLAFUR
GERMANY
www.olafureliasson.net
Olafur Eliasson
"Analemma for
Kunsthaus Zug,"
2009, Courtesy of
Kunsthaus Zug,
© 2009 Olafur
Eliasson
PP : 60-61

/ F

FAKHAMZADEH, BABAK
BRAZIL
www.babakfakhamzadeh.com
PP : 8, 184-187

FEININGER, ANDREAS
UNITED STATES
PP : 228-229
Andreas Feininger/
The LIFE Picture
Collection/Getty
Images

FELTON, NICHOLAS
UNITED STATES
www.feltron.com
P : 14

FERGUSON, KEVIN L.
UNITED STATES
www.flickr.com/photos/a2050
PP : 78-79

FIORE, ROSEMARIE
UNITED STATES
www.rosemariefiore.com
Rosemarie Fiore
Studio and Von
Lintel Gallery,
Los Angeles
PP : 214-215

FISCHER, ERIC
UNITED STATES
www.flickr.com/photos/
walkingsf
PP : 15, 20-21

FONG, QI WEI
SINGAPORE
www.fqwimages.com
(FQWimages pte
ltd.)
PP : 26-31

FONTENOY, FRÉDÉRIC
FRANCE
www.fredericfontenoy.com
PP : 196-197

FUNCH, PETER
UNITED STATES
www.peterfunch.com
Images courtesy
of the artist
Peter Funch
and V1 Gallery
PP : 12, 104-111

/ G

GARCIA, JESSE
UNITED STATES
www.flickr.com/photos/
papajesse
To Sandy, Always
PP : 148-149

**GLINA, PIERO AND
MARTIN BORST**
SWITZERLAND
www.pieroglina.com
PP : 76-77

/ H

**HENSINGER, JAMES
SPEED**
UNITED STATES
www.JHensinger.org
Copyright © 2013
by James Speed
Hensinger.
PP : 234-235

HOCKNEY, DAVID
UNITED STATES /
UNITED KINGDOM
www.hockneypictures.com
"The Crossword
Puzzle, Minneapolis,
Jan. 1983"
Photographic

collage, edition of
10, 33 x 46 inch,
© David Hockney,
Photo Credit:
Richard Schmidt,
PP : 96-97
"The Scrabble
Game, Jan. 1, 1983"
Photographic col-
lage, edition of 20,
39 x 58 inch,
© David Hockney,
Photo Credit:
Richard Schmidt,
PP : 98-99

HOUSER, JIM
UNITED STATES
www.jimhouser.com
PP : 11, 52-57

HLYNSKY, DENNIS
UNITED STATES
www.vimeo.com/
dennishlynsky
PP : 46-51

/ I

IEPE
GERMANY
www.iepe.net
PP : 210-211

IRVINE, STEVE
CANADA
www.steveirvine.com
PP : 230-233

/ J

JL DESIGN AND KORB
LITHUANIA
www.korb.tv
Client: CCTV
Creative Director: JL
Agency: JL DESIGN
Executive producer:
Angela Moo
Project Manager:
Jennifer Lin
Art Director: Lance Wei
Designers: Hsiang
Ju Hung, Utsuo Chen
VFX / Design

IMPRINT

/

This book was edited, and designed by Gestalten.

Edited by Nicholas Felton, Sven Ehmann,
and Robert Klanten

Preface by Nicholas Felton
Essay and project texts by Kevin Brochet-Nguyen

Editorial management by Maria-Elisabeth Niebius
Copyediting by Victoria Pease
Proofreading by Felix Lennert

Layout and cover by Sarah Peth
Typeface: Blender Pro by Nik Thoenen
Foundry: www.gestaltenfonts.com

Cover image by Mike Kelley

Printed by Printer Trento s.r.l., Trento, Italy
Made in Europe

Published by Gestalten, Berlin 2016
ISBN 978-3-89955-645-2

Bibliographic information published by the Deutsche
Nationalbibliothek. The Deutsche Nationalbibliothek lists this
publication in the Deutsche Nationalbibliografie; detailed
bibliographic data are available online at http://dnb.d-nb.de.

None of the content in this book was published in exchange
for payment by commercial parties or designers; Gestalten
selected all included work based solely on its artistic merit.

This book was printed on paper certified according to the
standards of the FSC®.